D0858522

QUEEN VICTORIA

THE
OTHER
HITLER
IN
DISGUISE

Prologue

Hundreds of articles are written as a matter of fact by writers about British occupation across the globe in their glory days. It is good to begin this with a brief history of the adventures of those who occupied, looted, killed and destroyed cultures and civilizations across the globe in simple quest for trading or more appropriately robbing. The main question finally raised here is; why are the British Royals still respected? Or why are they Royals to everyone including whom they tortured, enslaved and occupied through the centuries. My comments throughout the book shows how these Royals and their ancestors were nothing but low life murderers even killing their own for power and wealth.

Some historical facts available on many sources and references provided throughout the book are for those not familiar with its origins.

For anyone interested in it; a lot of historic information is available on internet on a variety of sites.

Some Historical Facts

In 1485, 7 years before Columbus set sail, Henry VII defeated Richard III at Bosworth Field and began the Reign of the TUDOR dynasty.

Henry had fled to France after the Tudors lost the War of the Roses to the York dynasty and Edward IV became king. Then came Edward V and Richard III. Richard III took the throne from Edward V's sons, his nephews. He locked them in the Tower of London and rumor persists that he had them murdered (this should already tell us that the Royals are barbaric in their origin and not so Royal).

Henry VII was followed by the famous Henry VIII who broke with the Vatican and remarried several times (I guess they could do it because they were Royals or just immoral?). The Anglican Church (Episcopalian in the U.S.) was founded under Henry VIII. You can still visit his palace, just outside London.

After Henry VIII died, his children took turns murdering each other, (really and those were the priceless ancestors of the current Royals that we must respect? Wow!!) switching back and forth from Anglican to Roman Catholic for convenience until Elizabeth I took the throne in 1558 for five years.

She was followed by STUARTS, James I and Charles I. The British Civil War, led by Oliver Cromwell displaced the monarchy after winning and beheading Charles I. Oliver was followed by his son Richard.

The monarchy was restored by the Stuarts and they reigned from 1660-1714 and were replaced by the Hanovers. That family, which changed their name to Windsors, still reigns today. There were four Georges. George I and II were rational monarchs whose name persists in Georgian Architecture. George III was king during the American Revolution and was declared insane (Yes, I believe some insanity must be involved through the generations to carry out all those maddening acts!). His follower's name was Prince Regent and gave the name to the Regency period before becoming George IV.

When George IV died, the only living grandchild of George III (who was declared insane remember!!) was Victoria who was Queen from 1837-1901 (the cruelest and most murderous period in British history). Her son became Edward VII but many of her children married into and became Kings and Queens in Europe. One became Kaiser Wilhelm of Germany (origination of my first name which is Kaizer!!! Wow, maybe I am Royal too…ha ha) Then came George V and Edward VII (who married an American divorcee and gave up the throne). After that came George VI and the current Queen, Elizabeth II.

Quite a dynasty and quite a murderous family tree…….wow!!

The British East India Company and Exploitation of India and other countries

The British East India Company was an English company formed for the exploitation of trade with East and Southeast Asia and India. Incorporated by Royal charter by Elizabeth I; the East India Company was a private company owned by stockholders and reporting to a board of directors in London. Originally formed as a monopoly on trade, it increasingly took on governmental powers with its own army and judiciary.

A royal charter is a formal document issued by a monarch's letters patent, granting a right or power to an individual and not a body corporate. They were and are still, used to establish significant organizations. It was started as a monopolistic trading body so that England could participate in the East Indian spice trade. There were also the Dutch East India Company and the French East India Company. Portugal was a major naval power in the Pacific although it never chartered a company. Company rule in India was the rule of the British East India Company over at first on some regions of the Indian subcontinent. This began in 1757, after the Battle of Plassey which saw the Company conquest of Mughal Bengal. Later, the Company was granted the right to collect revenue, in Bengal and Bihar; or in 1773, when the Company established a capital in Calcutta, appointed its first Governor-General, Warren Hastings, and became directly involved in governance or beginning to rule parts of India.

Similar to the East India Company several other companies were formed to exploit countries across the globe in name of trade but essentially overpowering the local population and looting.

-Dutch East India Company, 1602

-French East India Company, 1664

- Hudson's Bay Company, 1670

-The Mississippi Company, 1684 and others to exploit the world East and West of European nations)

In 1857 India's natives revolted against the company and the British Government abolished the East India Company and took control of the sub-continent. India housed mainly Hindus and Muslims and they took to fighting each other. After World War II, a separate state for Muslims was founded called Pakistan. The country was divided in three parts with India in the middle. The Hindu majority in East Pakistan became Bangladesh in 1971.

Victoria, Queen of Great Britain, 1819-1901
Image: Public Domain. Library of Congress

Reign of Queen Victoria

It is difficult to believe that someone who went with looters, pirates, killers and guns and killed innocent people all over the world is still revered in modern time as Queen Mother. Queen Victoria and now this Queen Mother Elizabeth's descendants are still kings, queens, prince and princess. They are openly revered in person by Presidents of great civilized nations even today as they bow down and kiss the Queen Mother's Royal hands soaking in blood and stolen diamond rings and admire her crowns jaded with stolen and looted diamonds from across the globe.

Why? The record of atrocities of the British empire carried out during the rule of Queen Victoria and her father Prince Edward and then later continued in Queen Elizabeth's early life too is enormous. The facts are silenced and hidden because the most whites and specially the current Anglo Brits are embarrassed to even think about it. They cannot believe that such enormous robbery, destruction of ancient cultures and human tragedy occurred at such enormous scale by their ancestors. Essentially hoodlums from prisons and slums of England were sent on missions to rob and kill innocent unarmed world. The Vikings from Scandinavian countries as well as Spain and Portugal also participated in one of the biggest blood bath and robbery across the globe.

Pirates from Europe came to kill and loot
Image: New York Public Library

As evidenced by Columbus landing mistakenly in America while planning to go to India, they did not care where the pirates of Europe landed as long as they could get tropical food, fruit, spices, diamonds and gold for nothing while destroying cultures and human lives across the globe. They took it for granted based on their use of gun powder and brutality. No one culture or civilization could question them or get in their way without facing death and destruction. They pronounced themselves wrongfully as civilized and superior while naming the "natives" as they referred to them as uncivilized, untrained and uncultured barbarians.

The British lost their money and power to control their colonies after fighting two brutal world wars. Unable to control their colonies across the globe they retracted from far and near. In some cases such as in USA the civil war resulted in freedom from colonialist. However, in most places across the globe; the British made it look like as if they were doing a favor in giving freedom to the occupied nations everywhere while keeping their feet in many places for future economic gains. Earl Mountbatten arrived in India in the year of independence 1947. He came to fulfill the promise given before or during the second world war (partly because they were forced to use Indian soldiers in the war) to give freedom to India but purposefully divided India planned in advance of the second world war by cunning masterful Winston Churchill.

He openly called Gandhi a Naked Fakir (Fakir means a beggar essentially) (Churchill, the Greatest Briton, Hated Gandhi, the Greatest Indian by Ramachandra Guba, April 16,2019, The Atlantic, Global)

He said that except for being exhausted by the wars many Gandhis would have come by and no peaceful movement would have convinced British to leave a county very rich in resources such as India. British had little resources and not enough soldiers of their own to control a large continent like India any more. Actually, they were defeated but they sent Mountbatten to create a posture as if the British were giving India back as a gift out of their generosity. As I grew up in India of charismatic first Prime Minister Nehru and

The city of Candahar with British Army on the watch
Image: Library of Congress

the traitor Jinnah who became President of Pakistan. A million people or more died in the transition and division of India into two large countries and other divided smaller territories. Massacres raged throughout the country during the transition.

James Atkinson traveled with the Army of the Indus, Bengal Division, as Superintending Surgeon during the First Anglo-Afghan War, through part of India (now Pakistan) into Afghanistan.

Image: Library of Congress

Pakistan itself was formed in two parts with East and West Pakistan (now independent Bangladesh). The reason for such divisions was because the British wanted port access from the East and the West for continuing to exert their influence and bringing cheaply acquired goods from hinterlands of India. They wanted marine access even after "giving" independence to India. The partition was conceived by British parliament and cunning Churchill several years before the end of the second world war. They used not so bright Gandhi and cunning Jennah seeking power to achieve their own goals of transition. Gandhi's non violent movement was cunningly used during occupation as well as during partition negotiations to benefit the British whose involvement continued. Gandhi was fooled again. India was handed over divided and purposefully conflicted between Hindus and Muslims as if it was some kind of a gift in a ceremony and as if the British were doing Indians a favor on August 15, 1947.

Indian Mutiny The Assault of Delhi. 1857
Image: Getty Images

All statues of "Royals" and their names were slowly obliterated from everywhere as India began a slow journey to be proud India again. India was finally having a rebirth or waking up period. Gandhi was shot on January 30, 1948. India could have achieved independence decades earlier if Nehru and other young leaders' violent approach was used a long time ago. British used Gandhi's peaceful movement according to me to stay in India longer while they were fighting the second world war with a few and desperately diminished resources of their own. While Gandhi was revered when alive his influence has diminished and India has become strong willed modern nation with atomic weapons. What has happened to the millions of nonviolent followers of Gandhi? Not much visible in Modern India for all practical reasons.

Ever since I was a young school student in Bharda High School in 1960s near absolutely empirical Victoria Terminal in Mumbai; I wondered about the British occupation. I wondered how a small country from Europe could not only occupy such a large population of India and manipulate the people even into admiring them but occupy other half of the world also without any repercussions at all. At Flora Fountain I saw British royalty exhibited in statues and names of the more prominent streets were after some lord or the other. Even name of a large populated city was changed from Mumbai to Bombay by the British. Wow, isn't that daring in world perspective?

Victoria Terminal - Mumbai
Image: Pixabay

What if someone changed the names of London or Paris just for their convenience because Bombay was easier to pronounce for the British occupiers than Mumbai. Such was unquestioned assumed abilities and power of British empire which made me wonder what else did they take for granted?

I arrived in London in 1968 to study Tropical Architecture. Once again it was ironic that education in tropical anything was being given in London; not so tropical a country! I have always joked about it with my colleagues. London was already teeming with immigrants from almost every colony of British Raj (empire). Lot of the small hotels and small businesses were owned by Indians and other foreigners. Some of them had already been here for more than one generation.

While being a student in London I thought happily of it as a reversal of fortune and slow creeping occupation of England and its territories by those whom British occupied. I often joked about how we were teaching them how to eat the curry as I could see Indian and other exotic restaurants were everywhere. I happily in some silly way saw it as taking back or paying back. And yes, it is creeping through and ultimately the British are losing control of their own country in many ways. I talk about this later in the book in more detail.

I always thought as to how the British Empire grew large so easily and how they occupied from huge land mass countries like USA, Canada to the smallest islands in the Bahamas that produce anything at all that the British could steal or rob without anyone questioning them. It was rule and rob without impunity. This is how the British Raj or Empire grew. They even competed and defeated other European countries essentially driving them out of their world of influence and power. Yes, ultimately, they were questioned and driven out. However, during their occupation and tyrannical rule they remained royal and mostly respected out of fear or native stupidity. Sadly, such admiration and stupidity remain part of nuances and mannerism even in the twenty first century and that has aroused my curiosity partly and propelled me to write controversial thought provoking essays here.

If part of the native population assisted them and worked for them to make their rule and tightly controlled occupation across the globe possible than should we blame those few participants also? If the natives participated or feared their occupation because the British had gun powder while natives remained shamefully fearful with their bows and arrows than should we not blame the natives too? Somehow the British cunning and the power of gun powder allowed the absolute hooligans often released from British prisons to become lords and ladies of the occupied world. It remained an accepted fact and their anarchy and illegal occupation lasted decades and centuries across the globe. Our emotional admiration and display of nonfactual facts about them even now is on display and that propelled me further to write these essays as I watch people line up in Canada to wave at the Queen or TV anchors gossiping with such admirable attitudes while reporting events surrounding not only the British royalty but other northern European countries from which nomadic Vikings sailed to loot and conquer other areas of the world or shared the mayhem across the globe.

My friends in England think that 200 plus millions of Euros given to royalty to maintain their royal life style and living on the hog in palaces should stop. They don't believe that the hypocrisy of royalty should continue forever and tax payers' money should not be wasted.

The facts and calculations behind supporting royalty are entirely different. Keeping the Queen head of the currently reduced British Empire and token head of the English Parliament has hidden advantages. Royalty is an international trade by itself and they bring in millions of tourists on the shores of historical England and to its monuments.

London Bridge / by Louis K. Harlow.
Print shows the London Bridge from a point on the Thames River, with sailboats anchored on the left and the Southwark Cathedral in the background.
Image: Library of Congress

Every child grows up with rhymes like "London Bridge is falling down......London Bridge is falling down........" . We actually prepare our children for such experiences and in a way the palaces and the London Tower and bridges are important architectural history of the world. British Museum full of stolen goods from all over the world is worth visiting.

I still drink "English" Breakfast Tea (although England can grow no tea and they looted it) and often get carried away about reading who and what a Prince is marrying to;which future Prince or King is born with such huge fanfare across the globe. You have to admire British cunning for that even now. How, they have the world fooled and their emotions entangled in their world. These are some of the founding thoughts of my essays here. The essays here are not written for historical fact checking. However, I have not tried to make up the general commentary. It is based on literature and historical documents that I have read over a long period of time. The main purpose of this writings is to bring awareness among general public as the English citizens and the Royals both seem to have amnesia about their brutality and the world has not held them liable and put them in a shameful corner such as they have done to the Germans. My simple theory is that the British were arrogantly and knowingly brutalizing any and all lands that they occupied and their acts were not any less brutal than that of the Nazis. It is about time to bring a reckoning of their forgotten savagery in simple terms for general masses. Yes, there are historical books and records but I want this to be accessible to masses to bring greater exposure. For example, if you wish to know about British atrocities in a country such as Kenya than read a Pulitzer prize winning author and Professor Caroline Elkins' books and essays.

She discovered hidden documents and wrote about Britain's Gulag a definitive study of Kenya's Mau Mau rebellion and some of the ugliest atrocities committed by British on innocent people. During Mau Mau uprising the British raped women and tortured those who were interned in the camps. This alone resulted in death of 100,000 and torture of many more while the world quietly watched. This is a simple and straight forward example that proves my basic theory that Queen Victoria, her parents and her children were worse than Hitler. And this is the premise of the entire dialogue here. So is the question.... Why the world still continues to cheer and applaud or respect the royals? Why this fascination? Are we brainwashed and cannot see the blood dripping from their fingernails like we do in case of Hitler?

Kenya Colony. Rift Valley and en route to Nairobi. Mau Station in Kenya. Uganda R.R. [i.e., railroad] summit of western edge of the Rift Valley
Image: Library of Congress

I have no such great unique ability or aspirations to be a historian. All I want to do is generate dialogue today to discredit the royalty abundantly and get rid of the hypocrisy among us. Yes, it is time to say this NOW .

Other writers have very specific information on British brutality across the globe. Omer Asad wrote in Novemeber , 2016 an article "10 Worst Atrocities Committed By The British Empire". In it he details how people were conquered and occupied. The British Empire was the largest occupying power at one time of 13,012,000 square miles and governing 458 million people.

According to Asad, "It distorted its colonies with boundary conflicts, failed to suppress civil strife, caused deliberate famines and siphoned off economic wealth, inter alia." They also left a trail of death and mayhem in their path of which some British and other white people even now seem to have an inert racist amnesia.

On November 9, 2012 Shenali Waduge wrote in Sri Lanka Guardian and I quote "The British Empire was world's first global power and largest empire with dominions, colonies, protectorates, mandates and territories controlling close to 500 million people covering over 33,700,000 km, a quarter of the landmass. In 1909 the British Empire encompassed 20% of the land area of the earth and 23% of its population"

This book is a tiny glimpse into the world of royals and their blood thirsty crimes of murder, rape, torture, starvation and looting. Look at the royals now and please think what their forefathers did and let us stop pretending. They remain unapologetic. Do you believe that the Queen Victoria and current Queen Elizabeth were "capable of burning down villages to the ground, seizing and raping women and children or elders, hanging prisoners without trial, starving locals to death, infecting natives with small pox, getting natives addicted to opium and alcohol"...........and the list goes on and on.

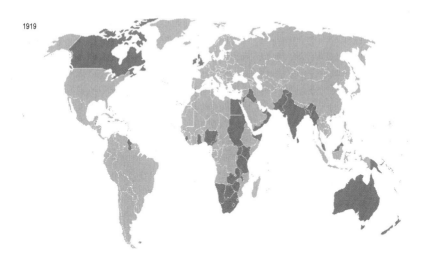

British Empire in 1919
Image: wikimedia:User:Gerrynobody

I am not the only one who is interested in revealing brutality and persistent "royalty" hiding behind falsified facades. My writing is a collection of visions of others and the history as revealed by scholars and historians trying to find and state the hidden truth under current illusion of respected royalty.

It has been often said and believed for a long time that "the sun never sets on the British Empire". Christopher North wrote "his majesty's dominions on which the sun never sets" which was changed to user friendly "the sun never sets on the british empire" Of course, it was one of the largest empire.

The Royals were invading hundreds of small islands to large continents under the guise of commerce while decimating the local innocent unarmed population and looting their wealth. At its highest level of conquest across the globe in 1920's the British Empire was controlling with their violence and thieving robber lords more than fifth of the world's population.

For a lot of these occupied population their sun was setting and never rose.The British Lords along with the Kings and Queens dripped with blood of innocent people more than Hitler ever did.

The Slave Ship
Image: Library of Congress

People around the globe were subjected to slavery, brutal killing, mass murders and kept in horrific concentration camps while their innocent sweet lands and households were systematically looted, sold and brought to United Kingdom or England. The British essentially invented the transatlantic slave trade to find labor for their and other European white nations atrocities committed on brown and black people of the world.

● ● ● ● ● ● ● ● ● ●

References
-Case Study; The Salt March by Nadine Block
-Britain's Gulag
Britain's Gulag: The Brutal End of Empire in Kenya, Caroline Elkins, Pimlico, 2005
-(Paul Gregoire, Crimes Against Humanity: The British Empire
First Published by Sydney Criminal Lawyers and cross posted on Global Research in July 2017)
-Crimes Against Humanity
Crimes Against Humanity: The British Empire by Paul Gregoire – Global Research
-John Wilson, Fun Trivia

Methods and Means of Occupation – the British bureaucracy
The Apartheid

The Apartheid one of the worst form of racism and segregation during 1948 to 1994 was established by British taking lead among other European nations. It was planned and approved under the British Empire. Boer republic mistreated the blacks and reinforced differences. The Native Land Act of 1913, removed blacks from their properties and farms and pushed them into slums of the small towns and cities. Yes, in recent times this has been thought out more often. All across the globe occupiers and conquerors wrote the history and brainwashed the young and the old to believe that occupiers such as the British were beneficent to their little island nation or even to a huge continent like India. Often it has been wrongfully stated how the barbaric occupier was so extremely beneficent to the "uncivilized" world nation. British history is full of it. In case of British they had to find a way out of how to make millions of "barbarians" cultured and civilized.

●　●　●　●　●　●　●　●　●　●　●

Civil Servants

In early 1800 Britain's decision was to give up on educating all "barbarians" but instead create a separate class of occupied slaves who would become interpreters and administrators for the British. This group of people in each nation or island that the British occupied must develop differently. In spite of their poor blood and inferior skin color according to the "royals" they must become "English" in taste, in opinions, in morals and intellect". For example, thousands of Indians were trained to administer for British people in other colonies outside of India. This necessity to connect to a few selected groups in various regions of the world, who would help them transplant their ideologies in the rest resulted in aggressively promoting Christianity and brutal reinforcement of Western practices. Thus, local religions, beliefs and ancient practices of day to day living had to be banned so the occupied savages can learn Christianity and the new or the "English ways of life". Those who adopted such measures and means were employed to lead small parts of the British Empire and given limited leadership roles in their communities to make others of their own communities participate in achieving British goals of robbing occupied nations of the world.

The British Empire created huge bureaucratic machinery to set up regulations, taxation and elaborate business patterns and practices to achieve their monetary and other goals. You can see and feel that in bureaucratic countries like India, Nigeria and the small African nations as well as the smallest islands even now that do not exist in the modernized nations of the world. They set up elaborate paperwork and misleading corrupt practices bribing a few and ignoring the millions to achieve their goals in trade of the occupied nations.

● ● ● ● ● ● ● ● ● ●

References
-Indian Civil Service, also known as Imperial Civil Service, Ramesh Kumar Arora and Rejni Goyal, Indian public administration institution issue
-Ranbin Vahra,The making of India: a historical survey

Occupation across the globe

A recent book by author Stuart Laycock "All the Countries We've Ever Invaded : And the Few We Never Got Round To" states that at various times in the last few centuries the British invaded 90 percent of the countries on this planet. He researched about two hundred countries and found that out of 200 countries around the globe only 22 were clearly not invaded. Often after a brutal invasion and occupation for killing and robbing the locals, the British did not colonize if they did not have enough man power in remote locations or could not carry away easily the local farm products and other goods. Some far off destinations such as Tajikistan or Marshall Islands among others were spared the grief. Also, the British failed or decided to make only small very easy to access and lucrative countries as part of the British Empire. The others suffered briefly through pirate like raids and brief invasions to rob and kill. Among such countries which were raided are Costa Rica, Ecuador and El Salvador. These small countries were raided using pirates by the British lords, king and queen to achieve their personal goals.

As per critic and author Jasper Copping Cuba was invaded by Admiral Edward Vernon who stormed into Guantanamo Bay in 1741. As per British practice of renaming territories he named the bay Cumberland Bay.

First, they were forced to withdraw because of "hostile" locals and disease among the British hooligans who wanted to occupy this beautiful place long term. However, after about twenty years the large part of the island and Havana was lost to a bloody siege by the British. Later on in 1763 it was handed over to the Spanish along with Philippines in exchange for Florida and Minorca. The British and Spanish among other colonial powers exchanged indigenous territories along with human beings living in it as if they were life-less objects of their thuggery and trades without impunity often in the most absurd manner as if they were exchanging toys or marbles.

The commentaries in this book mainly shows those territories under the British rule that were tortured, robbed and humiliated for a short period of a few years to decades and centuries.

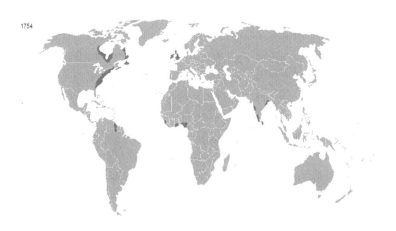

British Empire in 1754
Image: wikimedia:User:Gerrynobody

The occupation and destruction of India

The British Raj or Kingdom tortured continent of India from 1858 to 1947. Before this the East India Company pretended to be trading while robbing and acquiring products cheap and or for nothing. They shipped anything and everything to feed England and other parts of Europe which has no ability to grow spices, vegetables and tea. When someone says English Tea I cannot help but burst into a laugh. Such cheating and lying and than naming a product that they stole as English tea; and marketing it across the globe. Tea was grown in many tropical countries using slaves but not in England at all. It is a joke and a slap in the face to people of those islands and countries like India and Ceylon whom British robbed as if they were doing favor to the natives as they called them.

Starving poor Indians
Image: Getty Museum

32

In 1858 the East India Company transferred its cruel illegitimate legacy to Queen Victoria the barbarian in disguise. Suddenly in 1876, she became self- proclaimed Empress of India – a hugely populated continent full of ancient civilization, culture and riches. The iron fisted woman ruled India until her death in 1901 and then the current Queen or Queen Mother Elizabeth took over. Queen mothers or killers? Queen Elizabeth ruled until 1947 – cruel iron fisted ruler for 70 years carrying out their barbaric rule enslaving the natives and robbing the continent blind. When India was handed over back as if it was a gift to the locals, it was carved out into three sovereign pieces which became Republic of India the Islamic Republic of Pakistan and current Bangladesh.

To be able to dominate a large populated continent like India the British Empire created Burma an independent colony in the eastern part of India. Burma was kept separate for a malicious purpose by the cruel Empress of India and the British Parliament in 1948 as an independent entity to be used by British later. Wow, the British conquered by brutal force, ruled, and divided the nation of India as they felt like and when they left; they left it in ruins.

● ● ● ● ● ● ● ● ● ●

References
-The East India Company and its role in ruling India by Ben Johnson, The Times, 2nd January,1874

Churchill
Image: Library of Congress

Gandhi
Image: Library of Congress

MAHATMA GANDHI – DID THE ROYALTY, THE BRITS AND CHURCHILL PLAYED HIM AND TOOK ADVANTAGE OF HIS NON-VIOLENT MOVEMENT? GANDHI KEPT INDIANS CALM AND BRITISH RULED LONGER. GANDHI PLAYED CHURCHILL'S FOOL WHO CALLED HIM " NAKED FAKIR " (NAKED BEGGAR)

Mohandas Gandhi, a great man esteemed across the globe for nonviolent movement and philosophy was born in 1869 in Porbandar, the capital of one of the small principalities of British-ruled India. His father Karamchand Gandhi married four times. Mohandas Gandhi was born to his fourth wife. They worshipped Vishnu and the religion influenced by Jainism that advocates strict non-violence. Thus, non-violence was a religious belief and embedded in the universal eternity of life. Mohandas Gandhi grew up in it and his civil servant father who served the British Empire like one of those brainwashed rented "slave". He enforced in his son the virtues of non-violence from his child hood. Mahatma Gandhi did not suddenly invent non-violence; it was embedded in him. Nonviolence was part of his upbringing and part of everyday life. He could not pick up a gun and shoot a thief or a British thug even if he knew one. He could not raise his voice or anger against the British who had enslaved his father and his nation. Nehru on the other hand as a leader of congress party in his youth believed in fighting the British and getting rid of them from India quickly. On the other hand when British asked non-violent Gandhi to give them thousands of Indian soldiers and citizens to fight for the British involved in second world war, so called non-violent Gandhi loaned the British thousands of his non-violent followers!!! British were playing Gandhi at first to keep the huge Indian population calm while they fought the second world war while borrowing Indian followers of Gandhi to fight wars as they were running out of soldiers and resources to fight ugly second world war. Gandhi participating in a war to save the British while refusing to fight British for his own country? Why? Gandhi was easy to fool and the Brits could lie and play him. Non-violence in India was convenient for British. However, Gandhi agreed to fight wars for British. Is not that incredible for religious non-violent Mahatma Gandhi?

On the other hand, the concepts of "ahimsa" meaning no violence to all living beings including to animals, a cow to a cockroach was the kind of tolerance embedded in Gandhi from his childhood by his parents, family and the community. He was vegetarian and believed in self-purification. All of these in his upbringing had impact on Gandhi from which a political non-violence movement emerged.

Gandhi was not a very good student in the school or the college. He did easily pass the Roman Law examination in 1891 in England and returned home as a lawyer or an attorney. He wanted to be a doctor but his religion would not permit it so he chose law. He talked about importance of education most of his life and encouraged children around him to go to school always. He was not very successful as an attorney in India and eventually moved to South Africa to assist a trading company as an employee. It is here in South Africa that the first seeds of non-violence movement were planted.

Indian Culture – Mostly a nation full of cultural and religious atrocities – Indian nobility?

Early in the book I want to acknowledge here that India that I grew up in is a country full of cultural and religious atrocities. This is important before I blame only the British for their atrocities. I am ashamed of my country as they continue to deprive the poor while enriching the few very rich families and upper middle class even now.

We are not so holy as some in the world citizens have come to believe. Yes, we have this image of a peaceful people, Gandhi, Buddha and Yoga that makes us look holier than thou. However, we continue to take advantage of our poor and treat them like dirt. The word "karma" is used stylishly in the West to define some kind of destiny but in India it means that you could not and cannot rise above your destiny or Karma. It has been used for centuries to limit ambitions and aspirations of millions by those in authority or the rich. There is an upper class which thinks of itself as holier than thou and they treat others as dirt. Poor live a life worse than that of a slave in middle ages even now. Rich Brahmins even now think their blood is upper class or noble and do not allow their children to marry all other cast considered by them as inferior. India after all has evolved through continuing religious as well as cultural clashes among different casts systems. The British Lords also took advantage of the cast system and created Indian "Lords" or "kings and Princes" to run the continent which was otherwise too vast to create and control. You can see this depicted in vintage movies like The Music Room in which an Indian Lord having lost most of his wealth continues to behave as if he is indestructible and at the end declares from where he descended and why it is his noble blood that places him above everyone in his surrounding communities.

So as I speak of atrocities of the British Raj the Indian Rajahs or Kings and Princes were not any different from the British Lords. In some respect the Indian Lords and masters were worse because they knew exactly how to use their "nobility" to treat their workers like no less than slaves in an effort to enrich themselves. The upper class or "noble Indians" or rulers inflicted greater atrocities on their own people than any foreign occupiers. When I was young and in India they would say it is cheaper to hire a woman house worker for a year than to buy a vacuum cleaner. Some of it has changed with growth in economy and education but even today in most large cities in India, you see poor living on the sidewalks of the streets and defecating nearby as they don't even have toilet facilities where they sleep on the streets and sidewalks under a canvas and their children go often to school from the sidewalks while the rich ride in luxury cars.

● ● ● ● ● ● ● ● ● ●

References
-The story of Gandhi | Students' Project - Mahatma Gandhi, www.mkgandhi.org
-Mohandas Gandhi - Bioraphy, Facts and Beliefs - History, www.gandhiashranasevegram.com
-Mahatma Gandhi | Biography, Accomplishments,, Facts, www.britannica.com
-Mahatma Gandhi Biography, www.biographyonline.net

Queen Victoria or Hitler

In brief, the Hitler's Nazi regime killed ten millions during a world war where there were conspiracies, deaths and mayhem on both sides who possessed weapons of mass destruction. In case of Victoria and her ancestors or followers all the power was on one side. They had gun powder while natives across the globe only had at the most bows and arrows. It was an unequal power using brutal force occupying foreign large and small lands because of their far superior weapons.

Hitler can be held responsible for a total of ten million people who were also contesting, competing and fighting him with equal amount of cunning and weaponry. In case of Victoria and her ancestors or followers they had an unequal advantage and cunning to go in "under developed" nations and in my mind innocent regions of the world were attacked horribly by British; besieged and kept captives for economic benefits of looting large and small populations totaling sixty percent of the world population at one time. British massacre and occupation makes Hitler's actions mostly acts of war with great racist horrific actions against the Jews. Queen Victoria and her thugs invaded countries who were living their own placid life and thus may be considered horrific acts against the innocent people of the world.

World has written, talked and extensively condemned the actions of the Nazis while failing to note or condemn the actions of the "royalty" and even tried to prevent it from diminishing. The reason could be as simple as this. Hitler was killing whites while Queen Victoria and her descendants were destroying and occupying for two centuries the poor " under developed blacks and browns called natives or barbarians" by inhuman British royalty .

This is what makes it important to open up the discussion by collecting information from across the globe of British atrocities.

• • • • • • • • • •

Columbus Day

It is absolutely crazy for anyone to celebrate Columbus Day. Columbus was nothing but dumb, drunk, bloody pirate who worked for the Kings. If you have ever seen Pirates of the Carribean, you will know that at one point they all rejoice nothing but their loyalty to the King and Queen of England then.

Christopher Columbus, discovering America
Image: From The New York Public Library

Columbus was an ignorant Italian born Spanish pirate sailor who by mistake sailed west from home with intent to rob, kill and loot India. He was supposed to sail East to India. If this is true than he must be totally dumb. Every day the sun rises and all you have to see was where the sun rose and where it was setting. When he arrived on the shores of the huge continent of America he still remained ignorant. He called the

41

American natives Indians because he thought he was in India. How dumb and stupid. Next what happens is a horrible long history in which hundreds of native tribes were killed and destroyed so only a very few remain on small useless pieces of land given by the descendants of the British Europeans the American whites as a token so they can preserve some kind of pride and identity while at one time they peacefully lived and owned the whole continent. Native American tribes were marauded because this stupid pirate sailor took a wrong turn.

Columbus statue was vandalized.
Image: U.S. National Park Services

The British have been brutal in USA and Canada. USA had to fight bloody wars to get the likes of Columbus out of here so celebrating Columbus Day sounds totally dumb.

Settler fighting with Indians
Image: Getty Images

The current calls for removal of Columbus statues from everywhere are result of his atrocities on native population. There is also a movement to replace festivities of Columbus Day. As I have said here Columbus was a drunk lout who came with his thugs to America while trying to reach India and destroyed thousands of innocent tribal lives and great indigenous culture. I also believe that the July 4th national holiday should be replaced with June tenth Day remembering the horrific days in Tulsa a hundred years ago when white racist thugs destroyed their well built neighborhoods during the Black Wall Street Massacre. They killed innocent people and destroyed a whole neighborhood for falsified reasons.

Black Wall Street Massacre and descration by white racist rednecks
Image: Library of Congress

After the well known killing of George Floyd by a policeman on May 25, 2020 placing a knee on his throat; there has also been great movement in demand for removal of statues and symbols of slavery and racism. In England where slavery was developed and used by Queen Victoria and her cohorts across the globe, the statue of Edward Colston; a 17th century slave trader was pulled down in the city of Bristol and thrown in the river.

In Rhode Island on Columbus Day 2020 the statue of Columbus was splattered with red paint representing blood. A sign was posted to stop celebrating the genocide. The statue must be removed.

Here is a horrifying example of how white racist think. Boston has had a statue of godly Abraham Lincoln. In this extremely impressive tall statue of Lincoln a slave is kneeling at his feet. Lincoln freed the slaves and than some white racists commissioned a statue of Lincoln with a slave kneeling at his feet. When will the racist in this country acknowledge that they committed horrible crimes against slaves brought here by horrific colonialists. Lincoln was a better person when in 1888 he said not to kneel to him but only to God! Changes are coming. There is once again movement towards compensating those whose forefathers were enslaved and used to build white dominated nations.

The Emancipation Monument in Lincoln Park (NPS Photo)
Image: Public Domain. U.S. National Park Service

Today, on July 1, 2020, Mississippi state officials will agree to replace the state flag which has confederate symbols. Similarly, NASCAR has agreed to remove confederate flag symbols.

More changes are coming and those racist Royals should learn from this to understand what changes are coming their way.

• • • • • • • • • •

The Golden Age of Piracy: The Truth Behind Pirate Myths, October 25, 2016 by Benerson Little the author

I have taken a lot of information from this book as it is one of the most reliable documents on Piracy.

There are a lot of stories on Piracy including a hilarious one in which essentially a decorated pirate Columbus travelled in the wrong direction and arrived in USA while aiming to land in India. The author Bennerson Little points out a lot of facts beyond the exciting and notorious myths generated around the pirates. Pirates essentially were robbers and they terrorized small and large populations. Also, pirates looted boats of pirates from other countries. The Golden Age of pirates started in 1655 and lasted until 1725 and beyond. They terrorized travelers as well as people on the shores of continents such as America and islands across the globe. They not only robbed but killed thousands of people. Often, they wiped out whole population of an island if the local inhabitants resisted even a little bit. Some of the pirates worked for their emperors back home such as in Spain and England. Pirates also came from Holland and Scandinavia.

While movies have popularized pirate culture and often romanticized it, the truth is horrific of what pirates actually did. We know of Marlon Brando the famous actor romanticizing with a beautiful island girl. However, the pirates mostly raped and killed. Also, pirates did not make the natives or anyone else walk the plank, they just tortured, maimed and burnt to get what they can out of the natives or other pirates. The Golden Age of Piracy is actually full of bloody wars and fights and domination of the natives in some of the cruelest ways.

Illustration depicts events of November 14, 1493 when on his second voyage to the New World, Christopher Columbus sent a longboat ashore at Salt River Bay to explore the Carib village on the west side of the bay and to search for sources of fresh water.
Image: Public Domain. U.S National Park Service

The Bahamas was one of the largest pirate heavens that became British Empire controlled territory with Nassau as a central large island for control of other islands. The islands were helpless and thus ideal for piracy and destruction of helpless natives in small to large islands. The massive ships of British navy could not ply easily in shallow waters and narrow channels of tiny islands. As per Author Benerson, "the location was also prime prey on the major Spanish shipping lanes which travelled along the coast of La Florida in order to enter the rest of the Spanish Main."

● ● ● ● ● ● ● ● ● ●

References
-The Truth Behind Pirate Myths, October 25, 2016 by Benerson Little the author

The Flying Gang pirates settled in Nassau.

Christopher Columbus first arrived in the Bahamas in 1492. He made a landfall at the island of San Salvador and he named it Watling's Island. He thought he had arrived in India! Some dispute this but Columbus encountered Taino or Lucayan people. In the area of Freeport island, even now there is an area called Lucayan which I have visited tens of time with my daughter from Fort Lauderdale where I live. The old history of death and mayhem by the British to me is only 30 minutes flight away!!!

Discovery of North America
Image: Library of Congress

When Columbus arrived in Nassau, he encountered estimated 30,000 Taino or Lucayan tribal people. Columbus began to exchange trading goods as he and the British did elsewhere across the globe. First do business and gain their trust and then take over. It was a simple theory applied across the globe. However, Spanish were there and they enslaved the natives to work in their farms and build the first residences and other buildings. This continued through the 16th century.

The natives were infected by Europeans who imported diseases. They died ultimately of harsh working conditions and diseases. They did not receive enough food or any medical treatments. Half of the Tainos died from small pox. The islands were badly depopulated and remained sparsely populated up to 17 to 18th centuries. Massacre by the Europeans of a natural kind was blamed on the unknown gods of the Taino and Lucayan people. Europeans just starved them and gave them disease but no known treatments or food!!!

The British attempt to settle in the islands of Bahamas was by a group known as the founders or New Providence and later on the island became known as the New Providence. It was a new providence for the British but not for the natives on the islands who lost their liberty and became slaves soon after and worked on the plantations for the invaders. They salvaged nearby shipwrecks to build settlement using natives as cheap labor. In 1670 King Charles II gave the Bahamian islands to Lords Proprietors of Carolinas as if it was theirs to give away. Those were the days when British took, pillaged, killed and gave to their entities how ever they liked it. An independent government was established and acquired exclusive shipping rights. The islands were occupied by French and Spanish during what is known as the War of Spanish Succession.

● ● ● ● ● ● ● ● ● ● ●

References
-For further reading, www.piratesofnassau.com

Destruction of native American Indians

When European explorers began to come to United States or North America their main goals were either to find gold or to start new life when escaping religious persecutions and famines in Europe. Before this happened, about 12,000 years ago from today, nomadic tribes from Asia crossed over a land mass that connected to from Asia to Alaska.

The first ship / painted by Joshua Shaw ; engraved by J. Sartain.
Ship of Christopher Columbus in background, and three Indians in foreground.

These nomadic tribes settled all across from the North America to South America. The nomadic tribe population was as large as 50 million representing hundreds of tribes. Christopher Columbus a dumb drunkard navigator arrived in the Caribbean in 1492. During this time an estimated 10 million native people lived here in North America whom Columbus mistakenly thought were American Indian because he thought he had arrived in India. Columbus and other renegade Vikings came with a mission of occupying the vast productive rich land and by 1900, there were less than 300,000 American Indians alive.

Bows and arrows against bullets
Image: Library of Congress

Some tribes were totally eliminated. Just in one area of the world the British occupiers killed more native people than what Hitler did to the Jews or the rest of Europe. The native Americans are now settled wrongfully in reservations by the American government deprived of their land which is now United States. The colonist staged brutal wars using power of their gun powder and killed millions taking their land and all their wealth. They took everything and created the beginning of racism otherwise non-existent anywhere else in the world. Land dispossession, starvation and blatant killings destroyed and dispossessed native people wrongly named American Indians. Columbus has been wrongly celebrated as an adventurer but in reality he became responsible for hundreds of years of destruction, killing and exploitations of the natives repeated later in other areas of world equally. He was decorated by the Royals wrongfully because he brought home looted wealth from across the globe.

• • • • • • • • • •

References
- Atrocities Against Native Americans, endgenocide.org

Puritan New England....Plymouth

May Flower compact and its people consisted of Separatist, Puritans as well as adventurers and tradesmen or businessmen who wanted to flee from the persecution of King James of England. On September 16, 1620 the Mayflower, a British ship sailed from Plymouth, England with 102 passengers who called themselves pilgrims. They are bound for the newly found world of North America. The Mayflower compact agreed among the sailors created the first so called "just and equal" laws for formation of the colony in North America. Intentions were good among them, their compact turned out to be a nightmare for the natives wherever the English or the British formed colonies as it happened everywhere. The compact was written by only the male occupants of the ship thus already not very democratic. In one respect it was a temporary document until a formal acceptance and approval came from the Council of England. Finally, in 1621 Pierce Patent was received.

Mayflower compact was important because this was the first document of rules created to establish colony or self-government in the new world. British almost always assumed even before they landed anywhere that eventually they will rule that island or country or the whole continent. They made up their own "democracy" and "kingdom" oblivious of the natives.

Plymouth colony eventually became part of Massachusetts Bay colony in 1619 thus colonies coming together to become a large nation of whites from England in USA while wiping out most of the local tribes.

• • • • • • • • • •

-Mayflower Compact - Definition, Purpose and Significance, www.history.com: topic: Colonial America, Mayflower Compact

Bahamas.

Many European nations beside Britain came over to participate in lucrative trade. The "Golden" Age of Piracy and the Bahamas Pirates were essentially thugs, robbers and killers who had no place or let out from the prisons of England to rob the world. Christopher Columbus was not a great explorer but a dumb navigator who ended up in wrong places. His biggest fiasco being America when he blindly claimed that he had landed in India where he intended to go. I guess he did not simply know how the Sun rises in the East and sets in the West. To British King, Queens and the lords it did not matter as long as he looted, enslaved and killed most natives so the British Empire can expand in all parts of the world.

Bahamas for a long time was a British controlled territory and a pirate heaven. The most notorious among them were Flying Gang and they occupied the pirate heaven of Nassau. From here they attacked Spanish trading ships and carried out looting and killings that remain unaccounted.

When this stupid dumb pirate Columbus landed in Bahamas he called it San Salvador which was also known as Watling's Island. The Bahamas were occupied by local Taino or Lucayan people for centuries.

(I often go to Lucaya from Fort Lauderdale to relax in our time happily and peacefully!!!) The Lucayan people had occupied the island since 1100's. They originally moved from the islands of Hispaniola and Cuba.

At first the Columbus and his gang started slyly exchanging trade goods with them as they did with natives everywhere to learn what the natives had to "offer" so they could later essentially rob and kill them if necessary. When Columbus arrived in the islands there were more than 30,000 natives. The British soon subjugated them to work on their plantations. Any and all produce were sold or shipped to Europe by the pirates.

Most all natives died of torture, killing and disease brought over by dirty ugly diseased pirates. Half of the natives died of small pox brought over by the pirates. Beautiful local young native girls were raped and contracted other diseases such as gonorrhea and syphilis. The islands which were happy and thriving until 17th and 18th centuries were now mostly depopulated of the natives.

During the occupation and the proprietary rule of the British, the Bahamas became a pirate heaven attracting thugs from all over Europe who raped, mutilated and killed the natives as if they were local animals. The British made Bahamas a crown colony in 1718 and gave governorship to English royals.

Woodes Roger the first governor was able to suppress uprising in 1720 and drove off Spanish. The islands were fought over by Spanish, British and Americans. However until 1800 they were fully possessed by the British. The local people were ignored during any fights or negotiations as if they had no say in the matter as they were tossed around between Spanish and British occupants.

• • • • • • • • • •

Thanksgiving – Really? A hoax Or an Invasion of Americas

I enjoy thanksgiving like all of us here in America. I want you to know that I married two European women and each has given me a brilliant beautiful daughter. Thus, you can see I am almost white…. LOL…I am not prejudiced against whites or Scandinavian Vikings who looted the world along side the British. Thanksgiving in my family has been a holiday but in context of historical events it makes no sense. We all participate in it blindly without mindfully thinking of its context and significance.

Mayflower in Plymouth Harbour by William Halsall
Image: Library of Congress

I have often joked with my friends across the thanksgiving dinner table about its origin. It's about how a mindless Viking or marine as the British thought of him mistakenly landed in Americas while he was actually ordered to go to India. Christopher Columbus a drunk sailor, robber and mindless killer landed in Americas and he thought that he had arrived in India and he started calling natives Indians and this is how the word American Indians still persist. None of the local tribes or its citizens were Indian at all. The English first arrived on that wrongfully revered ship Mayflower at Cape Code. Nightmare for North America and the rest is history.

I believe it is after meeting the American Indians and exchanging gifts – shiny fake beads for genuine beautiful corn and other fruit – that the British realized finally that they were in the land of abundance. They realized that the Americas were rich in resources and thus worth exploring and occupying. That merciless day when the English pirates decided to form a small colony at Jamestown, Virgina; was the beginning of a planned massacre and robbery greater than anywhere in the history of the world of any native tribal land. The cunning English knew that the Indians had lived there peacefully forming a variety of tribal groups and only with bows and arrows mostly used for hunting. The dirty low life sailors, robbers, thieves and prisoners let out from the ugliest prisons in England -the occupants of Mayflower and the first colony – felt strong and knew they could kill and destroy any Indian tribes that objected and slowly occupy whole Northern America as fast as they could kill, robe and control American Indians. An innocent beautiful land and its occupants were looted and massacred without much retribution or shame.

• • • • • • • • • •

-The Mayflower- History, www.history.com
-Mayflower and Mayflower Compact, www.plimoth.org
-Mayflower Story, www.mayflowerstory.com

Berlin Conference of 1884-1885 also known as Congo Conference Colonization and destruction of African nations

The Berlin Conference of 1884 which is also known as Congo conference created regulations for commerce with Africa. Germany thru such acts emerged as an imperial power. The first Chancellor of Germany Otto von Bismarck organized the conference which organized the general scramble for Africa. It resulted in colonial partitioning of Africa. Africans had no word or presence in such a conference.

Their faith was decided by the great Europeans without even bothering to think their existence at all. Its ultimate purpose was to conveniently override any and all forms of African autonomy and self-governance. Africans were considered non-existent and treated again like animals. After such an act many of the countries in Africa for one reason or the other were taken over because of great amount of wealth they could generate in form of ivory, gold, farming products and tens of other minerals. Portugal, Britain, France, Germany and Italy formed partnerships with each other and took over control of small and large African countries.

There is a lot of historical details that are being avoided but the main focus was on taking whatever they can without any questions.

Gun powder created the possibility to annihilate Africans like dogs when they complained. Expeditions were dispatched to either coerce local rulers and force was used to depose them or kill them.

This was all approved by European rulers or the Royal bloods of Europe. British conquered most land and caused most death and brutality to the native as they did everywhere. By the end of the conference, Africa was divided in pieces as we know it now!

(There are tens of articles and books on Analysis of Western European colonialism and occupation. However, main goal here was how to define a form of looting and occupation everywhere and then look good at the end.)

• • • • • • • • • •

-Berlin Conference of 1884 - 1885, www.oxfordreference.com
-Berlin Conference, South Africa History, www.sahistory.com
-Berlin 1884, Remembering the conference that divided Africa, www.aljazeera.com

The Slave Trade

How British Empire conducted slavery for 245 years

John Hawkins was the first and the most prominent slave trader. As early as 1563 he brought slaves for selling to Santa Domingo. During this period of British occupations in Africa they were more interested in looting or "buying cheap" agriculture products. Several British merchants were charged to carry away gold, ivory, pepper, indigo and other products. There was rivalry between other thieves and plunderers such as Dutch, Danes, Portuguese and Swedes. These European "merchants" -actually plunderers- came from all over Northern Europe under the pretext of trade. This rivalry also reached on the shores of America once the slaves to work under European ruthless powers were introduced. As per National Archives; the Dutch merchants introduced sugar trade. Barbarians or natives everywhere learned to plant and produce sugar for Europeans. The Dutch merchant supplied slaves in 1630s to the local farmers so that they could grow more sugar!! Those landowners and the suppliers of Africans classified slaves as property with a few rights. Such laws were easily adopted in other British colonies across the globe and specially in Americas. Britain transported 3.1 million slaves to the islands and the colonies of Americas.

The British became dominant only after the slave trade routes were opened in 16th and 17th centuries.

The British American colonies most abused the slave trades from Africa to the Americas and other colonies. Map below showing slave fort locations, catalogue reference and destruction of local culture and pride were similar as well as in nearby country India. This makes it very clear that the European and American television and other media continue to glorify British atrocities across the globe by painting a rosy picture of the British occupation and avoiding reporting their acts of murder, rape and looting across the globe. Just like a part of English citizens the media tries to make it look like as if British did favors by going to remote corners of the world.

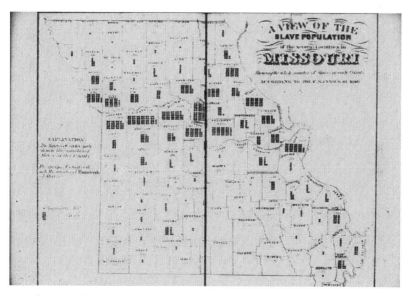

Map of Missouri slave population in 1860
Image: Public Domain. National Park Service

References
-Britain and the Slave Trade, www.nationalarchives.com
-British Involvement in the Transatlantic Slave Trade, abolition.e2bn.org
-British Slave Trade | slavery, www.remembrance.org

Colonization of innocent islands of Bahamas

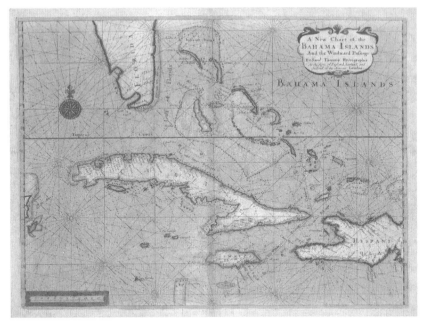

Bahamas
Image: New York Public Library

The French occupied Abaco in Bahamas as early as 1565 and than again in 1625. Many believed that Bahamas were not colonized until late 17th century. Colonization of such hundreds of small and large islands tried by Britain, France, the Netherlands and Spain occurred at different times in history. When Christopher Columbus got lost and stumbled upon Bahamian islands in 1493 , he did not necessarily occupy them. Similarly, Spain discovered them but did not occupy them. There was less wealth and less to loot and take home except coconuts and bananas! During certain periods in the history of Bahamas, it became a

The pirate Blackbeard (real name Edward Teach)
Image: Library of Congress

heaven for pirates such as the infamous Blackbeard during 1680 to 1718. British around 1718, decided to destroy the Pirate occupancy and made Bahamas a crown colony. Bahamians had no weapons or training to fight the British and thus they were occupied by pirates first and then the British thugs later. World just until now refused to assist the people in those islands. They were nobody in the eyes of the world and the British have always believed that they did the islands a favor!!! When Columbus arrived in the Bahamas, he wiped out entire native Lucayan population of the Bahamas. Wow!!!

Christopher Columbus landing in America, October 12th,1492

Image: Library of Congress

Has anyone raised any questions about it? Have the royals accepted any responsibilities. Not only the pirates but the English settlers crushed the island people to nothing when they came over to overly crowded island of Bermuda around 1647. The life in the island was not easy. One could live on some farming and fishing. The other occupation that became available was salvaging wrecked ships. The Spanish were not happy about that at all as quite a lot of those wrecked ships belonged to them. The other ships to salvage were those wrecked by the pirates.

Columbus' fleet endures a fierce storm off the coast of Honduras on the Fourth Voyage to the New World.

Image: Public Domain. U. S. National Park Service

• • • • • • • • • •

References
-Barry. JJ (1869) The life of Christopher. Columbus: From Authentic Spanish and Italian Documents; New York: The American News Company
-Christopher Columbus and Bartolome de Las Casas, Samuel Kettell, Personal narritive of the first voyage of Colombus to America, from a script recently discovered in Spain, T.B Waitand Son, 1827.

British Carribean islands? Occupation and blood letting

Even today we have British Caribbean or Bahamian islands. This is ridiculous as the history of occupation and governance continues many decades after the World war. When I went for a small project as an architect a few years ago to St. Martin island; I was told that it was half Dutch and half French. So, let us not only blame the British. Vikings and royals from all European nations had their own ambitions of expanding their rule across the globe. They sent out the Vikings and the mutineers to go kill innocent islanders and occupy whatever they could with cunning and use of gun powder.

• • • • • • • • • •

Trinidad and Tobago

I always wondered why there were so many people of Indian origin in some of the islands.As per Trinidadandtobagonews.com the Indians were brought from East India as indentured servants (I guess nice way not to call them slaves so just call them indentured servants without much choice). The reason was very simple there was not much population in the islands and the British needed workers on the island.

Africans were brought as slaves and treated like slaves but the Indians got a differed respect as indentured servants but paid very little for their hard work. Trinidad's population was very little approximately 2,700 natives. There were only about 2,000 Amerindians and only about 300 slaves in 1783. The population of those who were free non whites was about 295, most of whom came from nearby islands.

The first sight of the new world - Columbus discovering America
Image: Library of Congress

French and Spanish wielded power in Trinidad before the British. They opened the island to immigration in 1776 and some Roman Catholic planters came from other Eastern Caribbean islands mainly to establish sugar farms as the price of sugar was rising. The slaves were part of the deal. More slaves the planters brought more land was given to them. Once again human beings treated like worthless work animals and commodities to satisfy greed of the European looters. They were given land grants and tax concessions also if they brought more slaves. This dramatically increased the population. Now there were 17,700 people on the island half of whom were slaves. There were about 2100 whites who dominated the island and clamped down on slaves and made them sweat and work hard in sugar plantations. There were also about 4,400 non whites who were not slaves but most of them were indentured servants which was another name for slaves.

Following the French Revolution there was an unrest or revolts in Caribbean which were quickly put down. The British were at war with French and the Spanish and conquered Trinidad in 1797. Trinidad was ceded to British in 1802 and they established crown colony rule under a governor.

I recently dated a girl from Trinidad. She was a beautiful, bright and nice. She said, British wanted Indian servants to work for them so they did not receive cruel treatment like African slaves.!!! Wow, only colonial powers could think like this.

Trinidad and Tobago became independent from British Empire in 1962 and became a republic of Trinida and Tobago in 1976.

References
-Trinidad and Tobago History, www.britannica.com
-Trinidad, 1498-1962, www.carabbean-atlas.com

REVOLUTIONARY CHARACTERS – WHAT MADE FOUNDERS DIFFERENT OR NOT

In the book "Revolutionary Characters – What made Founders different" Pulitzer Prize winning author Gordon S. Wood provides definite concepts and details of who and what has made America great. It shows the struggle and achievements of uniquely talented revolutionary era leaders. He provides some astonishing details of what I am trying to emphasize that behind these great leaders trying to achieve independence and develop constitution exist definite stains of slavery. Accordingly, he talks about how Jefferson's love for and declaration of liberty, justice and equality leads to embarrassing revelation of his lifelong ownership of slavery. It makes mockery of Jefferson's public denunciation in face of his and his ancestors trading slaves and keeping slaves like little low life creatures to serve him and his family. He hated slavery but continued to enjoy what it could provide for his comfort and prosperity. He made attempts at manumission of slaves as early as in late 17th century but he failed to free his own slaves. Jefferson owned more than 600 slaves that he inherited from his slave trading father .

Historians have recently pointed out that Jefferson could not see blacks living among the whites. He wanted to send them all back. He traded in slaves like all his other farmers around Monticello.

He treated them like worse than dogs and hunted them down if they decided to run. He bought and bred them like farm animals. He paid them nothing except providing horrible living spaces and some cheap food. He wanted all slaves to be sent to Africa and West Indies as fast as one can. Emancipation was not even considered. Jefferson was just like any individual of his time trading in slaves; buying and selling them like animals, cheaper than farm animals. He was against intermingling of African, Indian and English or British blood. Lot of other nations which colonized black or brown nations across the globe were in agreement with intermingling the blood but not the British who – all of them – thought their blood was unique and royal.

Thomas Jefferson Home built and maintained by his slaves.
Image: New York Public Library

Jefferson became responsible in what some white Americans feel in racial mix up of a small percentage in our current society. Even today white parents refuse or advice their children not to intermarry crossing the racial lines. Some still say expressly with resentment; Oh she is married to a black guy !!! Similarly, some black parents advice their children to not marry white or Hispanics outside their race. Jefferson becomes visible in us often. Thus, thinking that Jefferson and his patriarchal foundation was worthy of any movement towards liberty, justice and equality for all is fatally flawed and questionable. Jefferson nurtured slavery and injustice privately and hugely benefited on the blood of the slaves while advocating equality only in words publicly. This did not sit well with those who knew him. His words about equality were more qualifying when it distinguished whites rather than honoring blacks and Indians in any manner or form. He was as racist as they come even in our time. He wanted to abolish slavery but not have slaves live among us. If he was alive he would be outraged to see what we have achieved out of his and other pioneer's words of equality; liberty and justice for all. I think he may be happy or he may just feel disgusted to see black, Asians and whites walking down the streets of the cities now hand in hand and loving each other. Jefferson's statues should be removed from everywhere.

References
-Jefferson's Attitudes Toward Slavery, www.monticello.com
-The Dark Side of Thomas Jefferson, www.smithsonianmag.com
-Jefferson's Views on Slavery, www.peplarforest.org
-The Enslaved House of President Thomas Jefferson, www.whitehousehistory.com

Boer War and brutal British Concentration Camps

South African War, 1899-1902
Image: Library of Congress

During the second Boer War around 1899 to 1902 the British held up entire local and slave population of mostly women and children in the concentration camps violating every human right. These camps were overcrowded and very little food was supplied. This resulted in disease and starvation and death. Out of more than hundred thousand Boers held up in such camps about 28,000 died of disease, starvation and neglect as well as continuing torture. An unknown number of black Africans who were considered less than human by the British also perished.

References
-5 of worst activities carried and owned by the British Empire, www.independence.co.uk
-Britain faces international war crimes trial, theday.co.uk
-aalthatinteresting.com

Australia…. Lies, KIllings and continuing "occupation"

The British invaded Australia calling the land "terra nullis" meaning that this land was deserted and had no owners. However, in later years, The High Court of Australia "abolished legal fiction" of terra nullis in late 1992 Mabo versus Queensland ruling.

Boer War prisoners held by British Army
Image: The New York Public Library

At the time of invasion of Australia there were 750,000 plus Aboriginals and Torres Strait Islanders living across the continent. The first invasion occurred in 1788 and the British fleet of thugs and criminals picked from prisons landed near what is now Sydney. In as little as 15 months half of the aboriginals population was dying due to smallpox epidemic that never existed before.

Bottles of small pox were brought on the ships and released among local population that never ever before experienced such a disease.

Right until the 1920s British massacred aboriginals of a variety of tribal groups like petty animals. Even Kangaroos and other native animals survived better and now propagated as tourists attraction. On June 10, 1838, the Myall Creek massacre occurred near Inverell in NSW. In this case the Europeans involved in the massacre were for some kind of a justice. It did not justify the massacre. 50 aboriginal men working for stockmen in the area were tortured. 29 men, women and children were beheaded. Seven of the European perpetrators were tried and hanged in this very isolated act of justice across the globe.

The torture and misjustice continues. Indigenous people account for 2.5 percent of the overall population. However 28 percent of the prison population even now of the adult prisoners is made up of indigenous people.

Australia was one of the biggest land grab under the guise of terra nullis as explained above. Its occupation began by bringing criminals from England who formed the first penal colonies.

● ● ● ● ● ● ● ● ● ●

Australia and the British Occupation (1788 - 1850)

Australia was a sparsely occupied land of the indigenous people (the Australian version of American Indians) and the land of Kangaroos that we have all learned to associate with as almost a symbol of Australia. Reading the history of the invaders and indigenous shows that the kangaroos have survived better and have been loved more than the indigenous people during the last two centuries and more.

This is when the First Fleet of British empire arrived in 1788 at Sydney, New South Wales, Australia. This is the beginning of early colonial period of occupation under the guise of "scientific exploration" creating the first small penal colony. Finally, it resulted then in creating more colonies and total occupation of Australia as we know now.

While most historians see it as European invasion and forced occupation of the natives, the British and some other extreme whites think of it as a settlement that did not result in destruction of the natives who live now their own separate desolate life hidden and denigrated from the enhancement of the whole "island" of Australia. British intent now in modern world are considered beneficial to Australia without paying much homage or care to the natives.

The very early colonization of the Australia began when a first fleet of British ships arrived at Botany bay in January 1788. The intent was to create the first penal colony on the Australian mainland. During the next decades the British occupied and created many colonies on the continent in a variety of water front from where European explorers found possibilities to venture into the interiors.

A camp of Aborigines in North Queenstand, Australia
Image: Library of Congress

British as usual did not send their best as they did in other parts of the world. They brought in 11 ships containing 736 CONVICTS from their ugly prisons. These were robbers and killers. Some British navy personnel and a Governor set up the first colony in New South Wales.

Before this cruel and unexpected occupation by thieves and robbers, Australia was occupied about 60,000 years ago by indigenous Australians who were made of about 250 groups speaking as many languages or dialects.

The first human habitants who are disgustingly called by the British as the Aboriginals first migrated from Africa about 60 to 70,000 years ago.

They settled in Australia about 60,000 years ago. They arrived on primitive boats and rafts risking their life and looking for new beginnings. The culture as the British call it about 40,000 years old was the oldest "civilization" living there. The Aboriginals according to all fragmented historical reports available were semi-nomadic. Just like indigenous people all over the world then. They were hunters and gatherers of animals and emerged in various location also as farmers. Europeans have occupied Australia for about 230 years and the government of Australia was formed as early as in 1901 thus taking the land of the indigenous people without their permission for nothing as the British did everywhere. We look at Australia as a country full of simple case of migration now as we view Canada and hardly pay any attention to the fact that millions of indigenous people were either killed or died of neglect by the British.

Australia and England are Commonwealth Nations enjoying close relationship and people from variety of countries have migrated in last fifty or more years. When I was in Sydney during the eighties for a brief visit bars and restaurants were humming with young and old recent immigrants. This made the city friendly but nowhere did I hear or see the indigenous people who have been killed or decimated by cruel neglect.

On the other hand, Britain and Australia are close and share the same monarch the current Queen Elizabeth. They share institution of Royal family proudly and criminal historical occupation proudly.

• • • • • • • • • •

References
Alan Frost, The First Elect: The Real Story, Melbourne, Black Inc. 2011
Page 76 - For Further Information, The killing times: the massacres of Aboriginal people of Australia must confront, Allam and Nick Evershed, The Balnaves Foundation.

Aboriginals In Australia - Where are they now?

The aboriginals who occupied Australia 65,000 years ago were hunters and gatherers as it is found in all ancient cultures. They had strong spiritual connection to the land, water and animals. There were diverse groups enjoying different spiritual belief and they developed skills as necessary for the natural surroundings they lived in. They are among the earliest migrants out of various parts of Africa. They may have migrated through certain areas of Southeast Asia. There is limited commingling among Australians and Austronesian people of later generations because of trading and intermarriage.

Before arrival of the Europeans or British anywhere from 300,000 to 1.2 million natives lived in Australia. There were no established record as aboriginals lived in small "tribal" or community groups. A cumulative population of 1.6 billion people lived there over 70,000 years before arrival of British and the colonization of Australia. The aboriginal population mainly lived in temperate coastal areas which are now heavily populated by a variety of foreigners. British became instrumental in the destruction of peaceful tribal population. The history shows that while British thrived, the native population died of smallpox outbreaks and other diseases for which no treatments were provided by anyone. In 1930s there were only about 50,000

Aboriginals remaining. Instead of thriving they were decimated by foreign diseases brought upon them by the British and others. During the post colonization period the aboriginals were depleted and forced out from coastal areas as the British built ports along the coast as they did everywhere else. The aboriginals started living in Great Sandy Desert not chosen by Europeans for obvious reasons. They now have small communities supported by the Aboriginal Heritage Offices in various southern and eastern regions of the continent. All in all Kangaroos survived and were loved better than aboriginals. Yes, both the aboriginals and Kangaroos are equally liked by curious tourists and often visited but Kangaroos dominate the wilderness and aboriginals are essentially extinct.

A Kangaroo Hunt
Image: The New York Public Library

References
-Aborijinal Australia; History, Culture and Conflict, www.infoplease.com
-Australia Aboriginal People, www.britanica.com

Aborigines before arrival of British
Image: The New York Public Library

From trade to investment and all aspects of life and they even use British accent when they speak. England is the largest investor in Australia and they share common military naval and air defense between them. The people of Australia are still British or Irish. 1.2 million of its citizens who were born in England are strongly patriotic to both Australia and England.

• • • • • • • • • •

African men crowded onto a lower deck; African women crowded on an upper deck.
Image: Library of Congress

British Inhuman Occupation of Ceylon 1796 - 1900

The British occupied Ceylon strongly between 1815 to 1948 almost the same time as India. During their occupation the population of Sri Lanka grew from 800,000 to now more than 8 million.

British were interested in growing cash crops and looting local wealth in gold and other precious metals owned by the locals. Entire villages were burnt and farm animals killed to grow cash crops such as tea. The tea and spices from Ceylon were in great demand and the British turned the local farms into slave camps. Besides the local people; Tamils from Southern India were shipped in as slaves to provide cheap labor for farms in Ceylon under atrocious conditions and torture never seen anywhere else including in the USA where African slaves went through similar torture and slavery. There were rebellions in Ceylon. One of the acts of suppression is known as Medulla massacre. The British crown gave orders to kill everyone and spare none among men and women except children under age eight. A randomly selected age number 8 !!!!!! Isn't that alone astonishing. This was of course around 1848 and not too many newspapers and media that publish glorifying views of the British royals existed then. One of the army general assigned there enjoyed breakfast while watching Sinhalese men being hung almost every morning in front of his residence. The other Lt. Samuel Baker specialized in hunting elephants. As many as thirty elephants were killed by the British soldiers every day and for their pleasure British designed bigger and stronger bullets and guns. That is a lot of Elephants and other big games killed all over the world for more than 150 years of brutal rule. Any apologies coming from Royals to the animal lovers in any countries? I guess some people kill others so why not by those nasty human beings let out over the world under vampire like dominance of Queen Victoria and her father.

The British moved into Ceylon from nearby India which they were occupying. The Dutch resisted halfhearted but gave into more powerful brutal British in 1796 completely. British at first partly administered Ceylon from nearby Madras in Southern India. In 1802 they decided to occupy the whole island and it became crown colony.

British Ceylon
Image: Getty Museum

British encouraged production of cinnamon, sugarcane, cotton and other valuable agricultural products that were shipped out of the island using local labor.

They introduced and enforced learning and use of English language and British institutions and methods were imposed.

Slaves just landed from a Slave Ship.
Image: The New York Public Library

British encouraged and sold land cheap to the coffee farmers as if it was a favor. Roads were built to the farms not just to help the farmers but taking the products out to the ports to be shipped to Europe for profit. Rubber and coconuts as well as Ceylon's famous tea were encouraged for cultivation. The tea was a big success and of course eventually it was packaged and called English tea so was the tea grown in Assam, India. Indian and Ceylonese labor was settled in farms and their blood and sweat created wealth for the British across the globe.

The British built roads and railways that united the island but the main reason they were built as in India was for transporting agricultural products to England and other parts of the world for profit from sweat and blood of poor people of Ceylon.

● ● ● ● ● ● ● ● ● ●

References
-Sri Lanka; Medulla Massacre, www.lankalibrary.com

British indulge in Opium introducing it in large amount to Chinese – Anything goes to advance trade!!!

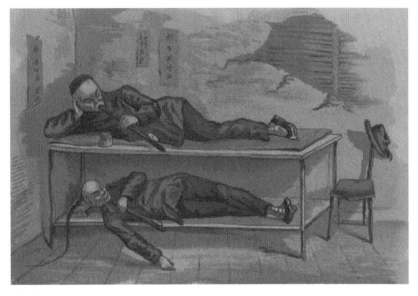

Chinese and opium
Image: The New York Public Library

The first Opium War between Qing dynasty of China and Great Britain was during years 1839-42. The reason is simple. Britain dominated the opium trade across the Eastern countries and profited enormously from it; the Chinese decided to ban the opium trade and threatened death penalty to future importers or offenders. This would hurt drug peddling by the British. Of course, with their gun powder and other trained help they defeated the Chinese and imposed penalties that gave Western countries privilege to be the drug dealers in the East. British never introduced opium in England or in the rest of Europe.

During such a war the British lost 69 men while the Chinese killed were about 20,000. There was demand for Chinese luxury goods such as silk, porcelain and tea which created imbalance for British drug dealers.

To produce more opium they started growing opium in Bengal, the present day Bangladesh. The British thugs were allowed to smuggle such opium into China illegally. The illegal import of opium drained the Chinese surplus economy of silver and increased the opium addicts dramatically.

Opium War
Image: Library of Congress

The Chinese government was concerned but they could not stop the smuggling of opium in their vast nation. They made every kind of effort to stop smuggling of opium. Lin the Chinese Emperor wrote a letter to Queen Victoria (my other Hitler and now the drug dealer too) and appealed to her moral responsibility. There was no response. The barbaric Queen dispatched ultimately the Royal Navy and they used their strong gunnery power to inflict decisive harm and defeats to the Chinese. Later declared by the Chinese as " gunboat diplomacy". The Chinese handed over or were forced to hand over during such a "gun boat diplomacy" some of its territories and Hong Kong. Now, we know how in modern times the British when kicked out across the globe (all though they claim they were restoring independence and freedom across the globe) handed over Hong Kong to China as if it was a gift. So now we know how in our times the residents of Hong Kong are rebelling against the Chinese to get their island nation freed. The drug dealing dirty British who acquired their island under threats and drug treaties benefitting their culture of looting across the globe had handed them over to cunning Chinese.

Treaty of Nanking is worth studying to learn how the Hong Kong remains in the hands of Chinese and people in Hong Kong are fighting centuries old tortures and misdeeds at the ruthless bloody hands of Queen Victoria. As one can see the British did not mind clouding up millions of Chinese with forcing opium on them and becoming drug dealers thus destroying a nation that did not recover for decades during that period. Are these really Royals? Or filth of the earth?

● ● ● ● ● ● ● ● ● ● ●

References
-Opium Wars; Definition, Summary, Facts &Causes, www.britannica.com
-Opium Wars, mtholyoke.edu
-The Opium Wars in China, asianpasificcurriculum.ca

India

Before the British occupied or arrived in India, it was the second largest economy. The British created divisions among local rulers in an effort to colonize more and more land. The new infrastructure if any was created to assist in British plunder and trade. Technological advances were kept away from the "inferior" natives and the control was placed in the hands of thieving British Lords. British ignored famines among Indians or natives completely. British commercial interest were depriving India of new technological advances as the British looted raw materials for their factories in England. Such factories could not find sufficient labor and thus the British employed the women and children at low wages creating huge problems within their own country too. Royalty was in charge of industrial wealth also.

● ● ● ● ● ● ● ● ● ●

References
-British Ray| imperialism, www.britannica.com
-British Raj Begins(1858), www.bcp.org.

Amritsar Massacre in India, April 13, 1919, Julianwala Bagh

Whenever there was any protest or uprising or riots against the British in India, gun powder became the powerful suppression. While Gandhi wrongfully preached peaceful marches and take the bullet quietly approach for his own people the British and the Indian soldiers hired by British as their coolies easily shot anyone who protested.

During a peaceful protests (thanks to Gandhi's nonviolent philosophy only applying to helpless Indians) against British Colonial rule on April 13, 1919, they were blocked inside the walled Jallianwala Gardens. The Gurkha soldiers working wrongfully for British for a little salary shot the Indians trapped in front of them. This can be seen, in a movie Gandhi. The situation was helpless and without any mercy and up to 1000 protesters who were doing it peacefully were massacred to make an example of them to frighten poor helpless Indians everywhere. It also injured and badly disabled equal number of another 1,000 or more. They were shot at within a period of ten minutes. The man who led such a brutal attack was praised as a hero and about 26,000 English pounds were raised to reward him! Part of the world if not the whole knew about it but did nothing because the white people ruled the world without any consequences.

● ● ● ● ● ● ● ● ● ●

References
-Amritsar Massacre, www.historytoday.com
-Jallianwala Bagh Massacre, www.britannica.com
-Amritsan, www.theguardian.com

Viceroy's House (film)

Movie "Viceroy's House" is pretending to be caring and beneficent for the poor. The movie clearly portrays how in face of defeat. British continued to pretend superiority while faking to care and attempting to be beneficent. More destruction was planned in advance. Gandhi and others foolishly believed that they had achieved great victory. In face of retreat the British again used their divide and conquer method by partitioning a great country of Hindustan full of 388 million plus people and the land mass of 175,000 square miles in three separate pieces of land and two religion based countries of Hindus and Muslims – India and Pakistan – against the wishes of majority of people.

● ● ● ● ● ● ● ● ● ●

References
-Viceroy's House is a 2017 British – Indian historical drama(film)
-Viceroy's House movie review, www.rogerbert.com

Treaty of Versailles 1935

Treaty of Versailles brought end of the first world war between warring European factions. It drained a lot of European nations of their power and monetary independence. However, these changes became beneficial to European colonies everywhere. British were drained from their resources to govern large colonies such as India and ended up borrowing money and soldiers from India and other colonies to fight their wars. The second world war had devastating impact on Britain. Churchill agreed to draw up sinister plans to divide up India. Earlier Churchill had said that a hundred "Naked Fakirs" meaning Gandhi could have passed by and he would not give up India. In India they relied heavily on local soldiers and trained bureaucrats to run their Empire. Someone in India has said that the amount of British about 10,000 left in India could have been killed by millions of Indians just throwing stones on the British soldiers. British governing power and their ability to send more soldiers had declined to nothing. However, dear conceited Gandhi was their emissary for keeping peace. Other leaders could not take violent actions against the British and they liked Gandhi. When Gandhi "misbehaved" the British put him in "prison" (it was actually a luxurious house) to keep everyone calm and crying for his safe release. It was such a joke. I believe without Gandhi, Indians could have acquired freedom decades ago. Gandhi helped British in bloody world wars by "loaning" them the best Indian soldiers. Shame on Gandhi who claimed to be peaceful and believed in nonviolence. Gandhi became hero but he played along and became British General's lackey. British used peaceloving Gandhi to stay in India with minimal force during the second world war but could not stay any longer after that. The ignorant conniving Mount Batten handed over India to Moslems and Hindus in three pieces- not two- as drawn up by equally cunning Churchill – the biggest lap dog to the monarchy. Of course, the queen and the other royals thought they were doing a huge favor to India.

• • • • • • • • • •

References
-Treaty of Versailles, www.history.com
-Treaty of Versailles, www.britannica.com
-Treaty of Versailles; An Uneasy Peace, www.wbur.org

Nigeria – a country ravaged by British

I was at the University of Lagos as one of the visiting faculty developing further the School of Architecture when I made friends with the Chancellor of the University Dr. Ajayi, a brilliant historian of Africa. When we talked about British occupation of Nigeria he aptly said "History is who and what they write". In case of British, it has been purposefully true as they destroyed a huge amount of historical records and distorted historical facts to create a glorifying image of the British rulers. Their descendants now portraying them as essentially the benefactors to the natives across the globe whom in reality they pillaged and killed.

On the Lower Niger, in the Delta
Image: Library of Congress

● ● ● ● ● ● ● ● ● ●

References
-Nigeria as a Colony, www.britannica.com
-Nigeria History, thecommonwealth.org
-British Occupation of Nigeria by Lil Bird, www.preji.com
-The british Occupation of Southhern Nigeria, www.digital.library.unit.edu

The Potato Famine of 1854 in Ireland and Corn Laws

Atrocities inflicted to the catholic Irish by their British Neighbors or Brothers

As per basic information available on Great Famine of Ireland and available in many historical books, more than one million people died of starvation and disease between 1845-1852. The population of Ireland was reduced by about 25% due to starvation and death caused by disease while British watched ignorantly without heart. Some people emigrated to the USA and others to nearby countries. This resulted in permanent changes in the political and cultural aspects of life in Ireland.

Great Famine of Ireland
Image: Getty Images

Ireland then was part of the United Kingdom. This famine created great resentment among the Irish against the British or English rulers. It boosted Irish nationalism and republicanism. The potato blight again emerged in 1850s. Echoes of pain from this era of famine can be heard even now wherever Irish emigrated leaving their beautiful country.

The history shows us since Acts of Union in January 1801 that Ireland had been part of the United Kingdom. Lord Lieutenant of Ireland and Chief Secretary of Ireland were appointed by the British Government and acted with iron fist on Irish land owners and farmers. Between 1832 and 1859 the Irish representatives in the House of Lords were mostly landowners and or sons of landowners like British lords.

However, there were cumbersome laws restricting rights of Irish Catholics. Irish Catholics were prohibited by restrictive atrocious penal laws that prevented them from purchasing or leasing land, they could not vote. They were not allowed to go within 5 miles of a corporate town thus restricting them from doing any business. They could not hold any public office and their children could not obtain education or enter a legitimate profession. These resulted in keeping the Irish down in the slums in poorly paid labor jobs and kept them in half starving conditions without any social or medical care.

80% of the Catholics lived in poverty and disgusting conditions. There was this horrific social pyramid. Anglo-Irish families owned most of the land and enforced their unchecked cruel power on their hired labor and tenants. Some of the Anglo-Irish land ownership were huge.

The Earl of Lucan owned 60,000 acres of land . Many of the Anglo-Irish landlords actually lived in England or mostly in London in vast palace like mansions in utmost luxury while Irish were treated like slave labor. The labor or tenants of such land lords were paid minimal wages for raising crops and animals in brutal conditions.

The British Government established a Royal Commission under Earl of Devon that was mainly made up of rich landlords in which tenants did not participate. However, their findings reported in February 1845 were astounding.

"It would be impossible adequately to describe the privations which they (the Irish laborer and his family) habitually and silently endure….in many districts their only food is the potato, their only beverage water…their cabins are seldom a protection against the weather…a bed or blanket is a rare luxury…and nearly in all their pig and a manure heap constitute their only property."

All of these disgusting things were done to their neighbors in Ireland. Based on this you can imagine and know how they treated brown and black people in Asia and Africa. People were treated worse than slaves and trashed.

Woman, on shore of Ireland, holding up a sign for help to American ships; her foot rests on rock enscribed "we are starving". Family huddled behind her.
Image: Library of Congress

● ● ● ● ● ● ● ● ● ●

References
-Irish Potato Famine - Timeline, causes and facts, www.history.com
-Great Famine, www.famine 1845-1851, www.theirishhistory.com

Looting Gold reserves of Transvaal

Transvaal War
Image: The New York Public Library

The British took advantage of the quarrels and uncertainties between the Boers and Zulus. The British began making claims over the local territories by sending more troops. In early 1870's the British interest grew as rich diamond mines were discovered. They used Africans as less than slaves to begin digging and based on the loot eventually formed an empire in South Africa. It was based on nothing but looting and racism. The British annexed Transvaal in 1870s claiming they were resolving disputes - technical words for occupying lands everywhere and looting the wealth of the region. In 1871 after the British annexed Transvaal they formed a Crown Colony.

References
-Transvaal/historical province, South Africa, www.britannica
-The First discovery of gold in the Transvaal, www.theheritageportal.com

The local chief was forced to accept only a few thousand pounds per year to give up his and his people's rights. Wow, what brutal threats can do to a proud native people anywhere?

Battle between English and Zulu, South Africa
Image: Getty Images

• • • • • • • • • •

Technological Advance

There were some technologies introduced by the British Empire in larger countries that they occupied such as India but mainly to benefit themselves. British are proud of having built railways in India. If you look at the routes of railways built by the British, they ran from the hinterland where cotton and other grains were grown to the port cities of India.

This resulted in India having fourth largest network of railways but it was not done to benefit anyone in India. It was a technology necessary to rob and loot India's hinterland without any shame and bring the goods to the ports to ship them to England and other parts of Europe for sale. Some British historians have tried to see it as some kind of a benefit to India. In reality, it destroyed India more. During the famines in the rural areas the looting continued while millions of Indians starved to death. These were mostly cargo trains initially to take the wealth of India essentially looted by the British to take from the rich productive hinterland to the ports than shipped to England and other parts of Europe. This is not because Brits wanted to give nice train rides to the local farmers. It was part of their looting tools. They not only took cotton, grains and spices but any valuable items that they could steal and rob often destroying old historical monuments. The looted items arrived in the palaces and some can be seen even now in British Museums and the jewelry and crowns that the Royals wore or wear now. When they make those silly waving hand gestures to the ignorant tourists who are impressed by their bloody Royalty, we all have to remember that the wealth of the world was stolen and robbed forcefully to acquire often every piece of that gem in their crowns and royal garbs.

● ● ● ● ● ● ● ● ● ●

References
-How Britain's Colonial Railways Transformed India, reconnectingasia.csis.org
-'But what about the railways?, www.theguardian.com

Slave Trade at Cape Coast Castle
Where visitors still shed tears and feel pain...

The British and other Europeans involved in one of the cruelest form of slave trade across the seas built about forty castles; actually horrific dungeons known as "slave castles" along the Gold Coast of West Africa which when liberated in 1957 became once again a beautiful country of Ghana.

Cape Coast Castle, Cape Coast, Ghana, Africa
Image: The New York Public Library

Cape Coast Castle was built by Swedish for trading in gold and timber mostly taken from the helpless natives for almost nothing. Later on it was used in trans-Atlantic slave trade. These castles were used to hold or imprison in horrible conditions in their dungeons thousands of slaves at a time.

Other, well known slave dungeon castles were Elmina Castle and Fort Christianberg. The dungeons in horrific conditions were used to hold thousands of Africans who were loaded onto ships to be sold as slaves in America. This is how the African American as they are "respectfully" now known as free people were brought to America. The castles were the end points in their native life and were known as "gates of no return" – a last stop before crossing Atlantic on an equally horrific shipping conditions where many of them died on the ship of hunger, fatigue and disease. Those who died were thrown over board like rotten dead animals.

The castles were initially used primarily for taking gold and mahogany from the natives in exchange of everyday use items such as clothing, blankets, spices, sugar, silk and many other every day used items. It is needless to say that the natives were cheated. The Cape Coast castle was one of the location where trading happened somewhat peacefully for a while. Later on the British found that human beings -the natives- were very valuable commodity as slaves in the Americas. Once that was realized the natives were gathered in the dungeons of the castle and shipped off to the Americas like cattle in horrific shipping conditions. They labored on the ship to get to their destinations where they would be slaves for decades and treated like animals again by British and the French and the Portuguese who used them on the farms as unpaid ill- treated labor without any rights.

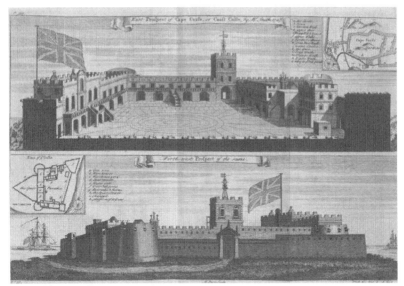

Prospect of Cape Corse, or Coast Castle
Image: The New York Public Library

Large underground dungeons were built in slave castles on the coastal towns and slaves were brought from nearby and the hinterland of Ghana and other nearby countries. As many as thousand slaves were held at a time in horrific dungeon conditions and some of them died while waiting and thrown out as unwanted animals. Shipping conditions were horrific and many ships drowned too killing hundreds at a time. The slave trade was competitive and thus it changed hands many times between several European barbarians.

In all of the castles including Cape Coast castle dungeons became "a space of terror" as described by many journalist and visitors. Slaves had no rights and this is the last dark horrific part of their life and they knew hat they would never see their families, children or their beautiful lush productive land again. The Europeans lived above and around the dungeons in absolute luxury and were kept well by other natives. They lived a luxurious life while the natives lived desperately in the dungeons and were often terrorized and died of sub human conditions and disease brought over by their European masters and exploiters. They were treated brutally and beaten often.

There is a shrine built on the grounds now over their dead bodies decayed bones and flesh. The shrine is for the local rock god Nana Tabir. The tourists who learn of such a history of cruelty often breakdown and cry while visiting.

● ● ● ● ● ● ● ● ● ●

References
-Cape Coast Castle / slavery, www.remembrance.org
-Ghana's Slave Castle (1952), www.blackpast.com
-Ghana's Slave Castle, the culturetrip.com and historytoday.com

Boston Tea Party

The struggle in the USA and India has one exemplary similarity. Salt march crusades by Gandhi and others eventually promoted struggle for independence. Boston Tea Party and the protests as well as the massacres associated with both of them in one form or another fomented the beginning of the struggle for independence.

Boston Massacre and the Boston Tea Party were both Colonial American Acts against the British that helped evolve The American Revolution. Boston Massacre happened in 1770 followed by Boston Tea Party as a protest event in 1773 about three years later.

A group of Colonialist who were drunk started throwing rocks at the British soldiers. One or two hit the soldiers. One of the colonialist was shot and the British claimed that they started taunting and shouting "Fire"!!!! Its hard to believe. The soldiers thought they heard a command to fire and thus started shooting more. That is briefly the Boston Massacre. This massacre and anger emerging from it resulted in Boston Tea Party. In brief the British taxes and occupation had created anger and colonialist were demonstrating. The British soldiers in possession of guns became responsible in massacre of innocent colonials. The British had removed taxes on most items except the tea to demonstrate that they had the power and control to do it. This caused the demonstration in form of Boston Tea Party and celebrated annually even now in Boston.

Same as about the salt tax in India, the colonialist were angry about new British tax on tea. The colonialist dressed up in Native American garbs, climbed into British ships and started throwing hundreds of chests of tea in the Boston Harbor. This was one of earlier expression of protests against British occupation and control same as what Gandhi and others did during the salt marches.

Boston Tea Party. Nathaniel Currier's 1846 lithograph of December 1773
Image: Library of Congress

• • • • • • • • • •

References
-The Boston Tea Party, www.history.com
-Boston Tea Party / Facts, summary and significance, www.britannica.com

Salt Tax and Salt March in India

There was also some tax levied in India by local rulers as the salt was essential part of food and its use in preservation of food as well as in other industries was vital. However, British East India Company started ruling local provinces along the coastal areas, and began to impose special taxes on top of the existing taxes beginning around 1835.

This brought a lot of revenue to the British East India Company. When the Queen or the Crown took over the administration of India around 1858, these burdensome taxes were not removed and impacted those poor people who worked in the salt fields. The Indian public were not in favor of such taxes that raised the price of salt. There were many protest by lots of leaders. The Indian National Congress raised issues of salt tax towards the end of the 19th century and the beginning of the 20th century. Indian salt farmers believed salt was a gift from God. Mahatma Gandhi went on a salt march called Salt Satyagraha in 1930 which is known across the globe like the Boston Tea Party. Gandhi said "I am shaking the foundations of the British Empire" and Winston Churchil said " The nauseating spectacle of this one time inner temple lawyer , now seditious Fakir (beggar)" Churchill lost this one. Gandhi was nominee for the of Time magazine's Man of the year. There were other such marches in many parts of India. Gandhi as well as many other leaders were jailed which created other silent protests. As one can see the salt belonged to Indians but they had no say in its production. Gandhi's Dandi March got world attention and became the point and method of protests in acquiring independence by protests of similar nature and creating a method and institution of non-Cooperation. Tax was never reduced. When first Prime Minister of India Jawaharlal Nehru took over the leadership the salt tax was temporarily reduced but was reintroduced in 1953 !!!

Gandhi
Image: The New York Public Library

● ● ● ● ● ● ● ● ● ● ●

References
-Salt March, www.history.com
-Salt March / www.britannica.com
-Salt Problems and Salt March, www.mkgandhi.com

Occupation of Egypt

Egypt was occupied during 1882 at the end of another brutal attack brought on by British in the Anglo-Egyptian War. This ended in 1956 when the last British forces withdrew in accordance with the Anglo-Egyptian agreement of 1954 after the Suez Canal. British were there and only withdrew after their own strategies for trade survived and could not continue. Suez Canal was important to them.

The reason British left was very simple. Although the British Empire achieved largest territorial occupation at the time of World War 1, British were no longer the world's largest and strongest industrial or military power. First the world war I and then the world war II depleted the British resources. They borrowed to survive but they had to withdraw troops and borrowed other countries soldiers such as even from India where "nonviolent" Gandhi gave Indian troops to fight for British and kill others rampantly using "nonviolent" Gandhi's followers! How can he be nonviolent and ask other Indians to go fight wars for British who were occupying India and he had set up nonviolent movement to remove British? Is there something missing in that so called "nonviolent" Gandhi in his loin clothes spinning cotton while becoming a war supplier for his own occupiers?

• • • • • • • • • •

British were not the only looters of India

As the world very well knows, the British were not the only looters and occupants of India and other parts of the world. There were other greedy nations of the European origins who arrived in India to carry out trade first and then occupied in one way or the other. The purpose was not trade but robbing and looting the so called native barbarians. For example, the French were in West Africa where they also learned to eat snails that they call escargot! Now, the world eats escargot and thinks it is a delicacy by the French!!!

In India alone, the Dutch were there between 1605-1825. Danish came to India in 1620 and left in 1869. These were the Vikings of the world. Their royalty also taking pride should be ashamed of themselves. French came to India around 1668 and left as late as 1954. Some of this so called trading partners were in limited areas of India. Their intentions were unclean. They sent criminals of their countries to do the dirty work for their own unique royalties.

Portuguese had one of the longest occupation in small western coastal areas of Goa from as early as 1434 ending in as late as 1961 beyond the British rule. They were less ambitious and did not proliferate as much as British.

There was rivalry and sense of control on both sides. Portuguese were more gentle and they also created their own style of architecture around Goa and Panjeem areas of the southwest coast.

East India company arrived in India in 1612 to loot under pretense of trading and occupied India and the British rule lasted the longest. They occupied most of India until the partition and independence of India and Pakistan in 1947.

Rescued famine sufferers awaiting food - government relief, Ahmedabad, India
Image: Library of Congress

Churchill had decided many years before the war ended in 1945 to divide up India in to three parts. He had a map already waiting to be executed after the war. As much as Gandhi and his party would like to take credit, historians and critics acknowledge that the two world war took toll on the British economy and they found it difficult to continue to survive while carrying out British Rule elsewhere. Britain was indebted by borrowing from everywhere including India. Britain's sterling debts around the globe amounted to 3.4 billion English pounds.

They owed India 1.3 billion pounds equivalent of $US 74 billions in 2020 money. Britain was essentially broke after the second world war. Churchill hated India as it became difficult to govern such a large country and its growing population. Most of the British army during the war as well as borrowed Indian army was engaged in the world war in Europe and elsewhere. India had many famines but in 1943 as much as four million Bengalis starved to death. Quite a large amount of food from such areas was diverted to British soldiers during the war and other European countries that supported Britain. Deadly famines swept through India in 1943 around the world war chaos and tensions:

Churchill arrogantly said "I hate Indians. They are a beastly people with a beastly religion. The famine was their own fault breeding like rabbits."

This clearly shows how the high up and lower level appointed British commanders thought of India. The treatments of Indians was worse than rabbits and they were allowed to starve knowingly by taking food away from their homeland and local areas. This is not something even Hitler would have thought. Here is Churchill so much admired by the world allowing Indians to die like rats so he and his soldiers can be well fed.

Partition of India – a final death nail by the by King George VI and his cousin Lord Louis Francis Albert Victor Mountbatten the last Viceroy of British government was due to bankruptcy fighting World War II and fighting Hitler. **Hitler's crime in Europe seem petty when you think of what British did across the globe.**

Mountbatten was great grandson of the evil Queen Victoria. He did not care about India. He mainly came to divide up India and leave to develop his own naval career back home. His hurried actions resulted in one million deaths and displacement of 100 million people of India. The British as per a plan drawn by Churchill and others broke up the Indian subcontinent in three parts. Two parts of the huge continent; the Bengal in the East and Punjab in the West were torn out to become Pakistan to please Jinnah. There was no hope of Federated India which would have allowed power sharing between Hindus and the Muslims. The evil Queen Victoria's grandson designed and created mayhem.

Poorly made maps were used to create two countries. Such ideas were conceived to continue the British influence for business autonomy in the two nations for years to come. Mountbatten brought in an ignorant Cyril Radcliffe a barrister or a lawyer who knew nothing about vast and complex lands of India. Mountbatten ordered him to achieve the partition and divide up Indians in five weeks drawing haphazard maps.

The Indians wondered which town and which village will be in India or which family will have to move hundreds of miles away to be on the right side or in the right Muslim or Hindu country. Once again British were treating Indians like animals. Radcliffe was able to complete the maps of India one day before the set date for partition. None of the Indian leaders were ever invited to discuss the territories of the two nations. The uncertain and cruel methods used in drawing up maps by a British resulted in chaos and mayhem. Mountbatten was more interested in creative festivities of handing over India as if it was a big gift. There was a charade to show how British were magnificent and generous in giving India back to Indians. Wow, after looting and torturing India for two centuries they were giving back to Indians their own country. Only the British can make a fully devised mayhem of partition to their advantage and glory. Mountbatten a spoiled grandson of evil Victoria played a central role and kept smiling while hiding planned mayhem.

As author Nisid Hajari reports in "Midnight's Furies" the bloody mayhem emerges before our eyes " some **British soldiers and journalists who had witnessed Nazi death camps, claimed partition's brutalities were worse : pregnant women had their breasts cut off and babies hacked out of their bellies, infants were found literally roasted on spits."**

All of these could have been avoided if Indian leaders were given upfront information and partition maps. They could have carried out the task more intelligently moving less of the population and achieving the partition in slow and cohesive manner. Grandson of Queen Victoria outdid his grandma for sure in thinking of millions of Indians as nothing but rats.

(derived partly from Adil Najam's writings "How a British Royal's monumental errors made India's partition more painful", August 15, 2017)

• • • • • • • • • •

References
-Portuguese in India, www.britannica.com
-Timeline of Portuguese as a Trader and Ruler in India, www.jagranjosh.com
-Portuguese India, www.newworldencyclopedia.com
-Arrival of French and establishment of French East India, www.jagranjosh.com
-French East India Company, www.britannica.com

Kenya and the example of British brutality against Mau Mau

Author Philip Murphy in his recent article dated October 23, 2016, "How much did British cover up its brutal campaign against Kenya's Mau Mau?" brings to light how British were clever at covering up their brutal acts against innocent natives. Of course, the story at once is heart breaking while British hid thousands of documents. If it is true in Kenya than it is true in most other places as we all perceive. The facts and records either did not exist or were destroyed by the British rulers locally. The British would occasionally torch the documents, reports and photographs to cover up their brutal acts. The Harvard historian Caroline Elkins interviewed hundreds of Kenyans and discovered "a murderous campaign that left tens of thousands, perhaps hundreds of thousands, dead". Elkins believed that the British suffered from amnesia when it came to their brutal torturous acts. Kikuyu tribe joined the Mau Mau revolt and the British soldiers detained thousands of them and maimed and killed equally. Kikuyu women and children were detained in their villages in hundreds of barbed wire compounds. In those brutal camps Kikuyu according to Elkins " suffered forced labor, disease, starvation, torture, rape and murder". Elkins called this institution of **"Britain's gulag" is definitely nothing to be proud of as it was nothing but a criminal act equal to that instituted against the Jews in Germany.**

Men of the Kikayu tribe, British East Africa
Image: Library of Congress

If Germany is ashamed of it or has been made to be ashamed of it than why the world has ignored Kikuyu's demands for effective reparations or why isn't it not wildly known? Is it because Churchill and the other lords thought of them as animals as British have often referred to those in Africa and the Asian subcontinents. **Are not such acts worse than those committed by Hitler under Queen Elizabeth that still garners respect among masses of people across the globe.** This is really the question I raise in these essays and with resounding why time and again. I now raise this question, why the descendants of such English men; common or royal; are failing to acknowledge this and take responsibility instead of being in admiration of their colonial rule.

• • • • • • • • • •

References
-Mau Mau uprising, www.bbc.com
-Mau Mau | Kenyan, Political movement, www.britannica.com
-The Mau Mau Rebellion, www.bu.com
-Mau Mau (1592-1960), www.blackpast.com

Second World war and starvation of Indian Population by Churchill

As I mentioned before Churchill openly called Gandhi a naked Fakir. The British among themselves laughed at his peaceful policies which were in their favor.

Famine Victims - India
Image: Library of Congress

During the first and second world war British were without sufficient resources or the armed men to control a lot of the colonies. Gandhi helped British by carrying out peaceful marches instead of taking the armed struggle to the thinly marginalized army of the weakened British empire. A recent YouGov poll found that only 43 percent of British believed that British Empire was good and useful 44 percent were proud of Britain's history of colonialism.

However, the rest had either a very negative opinion or remain non expressive. It is the same now among people everywhere who think current expressions of Royalty are not good. The robbery, cruelty and starvation in India and around the world was devastating.

They even "deindustrialized" Indian fabric industry in Bengal because it was not in British interest. They forced Bengalis not to weave any fabric and took the cotton to England to develop their own factories and in the process put local population to forced starvation. They brought in cheap fabric from England and forced it upon local population thus putting Bengali fabric industry workers out of work and forcing starvation. The cotton like tea grew in India but British now owned it and just like English tea the English cotton was fabricated and marketed to the world putting local weavers out of business.

12 to 29 million people were starved in India alone during this period. Compare that to Hitler killing six million Jews and another 4 million during the world war. Hitler has been condemned but the brutal Queen the other Hitler and her descendants are respected and revered.

The Orissa famine of 1866 is well known as the Queen and her lords and army watched one in three local people perished in the famine. The region's hundreds of years old textile industry was killed by the British occupation thus becoming responsible for the starvation.

More and more people were pushed into agriculture growing food and cotton, becoming dependent entirely on local monsoon and thus starving during dry spell with no help from the British occupiers. The British explained that the famine was nature's way of responding to overpopulation as if human beings were worse than kettle or chicken which were well fed and taken care of so the brutal English thugs can feed themselves while poor Indians starved to their death!!!

Independence and Partition – some simple lines drawn along religious line causing one million or more deaths......How Churchill who called Gandhi a naked Fakir planned this years ago before British left?

• • • • • • • • • •

References
-How British let one million Indians die of famine, www.bbc.com
-Orissa Famine of 1866, www.jstar.org
-The Great Orissa Famine of 1866, www.historyofodisha.in

Sierra Nevada

The Queen Victoria and her follower thugs from prisons of Britain moved into East Africa and Kenya by 1920 was declared the Crown colony. The past and current royalty wants you to believe as they did elsewhere that this was a trading post but in reality this was a murderous robbery intended armed invasion.

After about half a century of brutal occupation of their land, the country's largest ethnic group Kikuyu rebelled forming the Mau Mau movement who opposed the colonial rule. Mau Mau fought against the British and killed some British soldiers in small wars. In October 1952, then Governor Evelyn Baring a brutal British thug declared a state of emergency that only lasted for a few years.

Kenya Colony. Nairobi. Saddler Street
Image: Library of Congress

128

Out of 1.5 million who suffered atrocities and death. Only 5,000 survivors who demanded payments for their suffering received 3,800 English pound in 2013 because of a lot of noise made by these people and some conscientious British writers. This was a tiny amount that only the cruel British can think was any kind of compensation at all.

Kozi tribe hidden high up in the mountains of Sierra Nevada escaped the British thugs. Kozi believe that the technology is destroying our world and the nature. They are not in favor of advance in technology and remain one of the very few tribes across the globe who live with nature and have survived an indigenous life untouched by the colonialist.

The Queen Victoria and her follower thugs from prisons of Britain moved into East Africa and Kenya by 1920 was declared the Crown colony. The past and current royalty wants you to believe as they did elsewhere that this was a trading post but in reality this was a murderous robbery and intended armed invasion.

● ● ● ● ● ● ● ● ● ●

References
-Sierra Leone-New World Encyclopedia
-Sierra Leone-British West Africa, www.britannica.com

18th Century

By the eighteenth century Britain was in control of half the world and had emerged from the chaos of civil wars at home of the seventeenth century. A small island in Europe with only a tiny population of the world was becoming a huge commercial and military ruling power across Asia and developing its presence in South Africa, India and Australia. Any port in the world that the British arrived they brought enough monetary influence and gun powder to eventually control the local "governments" and "institutions". The eighteenth century English "fiscal-military" history, according to historian James Brewer could mobilize wealth and wage war as no state in history ever had (John Brewer, Sinews of Power:War, Money and the English State, 1688-1783, (new York, Knopf, 1989)

Old Dockyard at Deptford
Image: Wikimedia Comments

On American continent it was Hamilton and not Madison who decided to turn the United States into a modern fiscal and military power in the image of the British Empire and France. The current America the super power as everyone of its President pronounces now here and again and again was built on such principles of money, greed and military power threatening and dividing the world as British did in their rising Empire two centuries ago. America has been smart in not physically occupying the world but only thru its monetary, industrial needs and military influence.

• • • • • • • • • •

References
-Revolutionary War, history.com
-Overview of the American Revolutionary War, www.battlefields.org
-Overview of the American Revolutionary War, www.ushistory.com

University of Pennsylvania – My Alma mater and its associations with slavery brought here by the British

When I was trying to come to USA, I applied for top Ivy league universities here for admission. Princeton and Penn admitted me as I already had a graduate diploma from Architects Association School in London. It was very curious time in America then as the south was still struggling from race riots and racism was widely practiced in most parts of South.

University of Pennsylvania
Image: Library of Congress

I liked Penn and now I like it suddenly more because the history students there have been intensely involved in the Penn Slavery Project, November, 2017.

I am quoting below some items briefly from the report written by Brook Krancer, Penn Slavery Project, Independent Study under the Direction of Prof. Kathleen M. Brown, Department of History, University of Pennsylvania, November, 2017

-The researchers learned at first about history of Philadelphia's black community from books such as Freedom by Degrees by Gary Nash and Jean Soderlund, Liberty's Prisoners by Jen Manion, and The Struggle Against Slavery Waldstand Runaway America by David Waldstreicher. They also studied Forging Freedom by Gary Nash. Nash's writing helped them most.

-They learned quickly that Penn's original trustees owned slaves.
-They tried to find out if the slaves lived on Penn's campus or nearby.
-They tried to learn what kind of life enslaved blacks had on or around campus
-Those trustees who did not own slaves were often involved in slave trading
-They carried out commercial activities using slaves such as while trading with West Indies.

-This raised questions as to what extent Penn's early funding was tied to slave trade

-It raised questions as to what happened to the slaves when they died or when they were freed after the Gradual Abolition Act of 1780?

-They researched biographies of Penn's trustees and professors when and if available

-Except for one trustee they could not definitely tell which others may be keeping slaves. The rich were definitely involved in trading that required use of slaves.

-One of the trustees William Allen freed slaves on his death stating " I do hereby manumit and make free all of my Negro Slaves" He died in 1780 so this is more than 240 years ago.

- In case of another trustee John Caldwalader he left "three male and three female negro servants" to his wife as per records available in the University Archives He left the remaining slaves to his daughters.

Those who executed his trust or will got " a sufficient number of negroes"

There were several finding by these student researchers that clearly proves primitive atrocities of the past and that most elite among the high society and with great visions of educating others they exploited hundreds of slaves and traded and treated them like animals.

These are the same people who proclaimed " liberty throughout the land unto all the inhabitants thereof" on Liberty Bell that still hangs in Philadelphia. The negro slaves were not humans but creatures worse than the animals. Benjamin Franklin an early trustee owned slaves for many years and later in his life became the leader of the abolition movement.

I think this sheds a lot of light on what other rich slave traders and others across the good old America were doing. Traders kept slaves locked up in tiny spaces and the slaves often contracted diseases and faced starvation and careless human treatment. If a university trustee or a professor was "keeping" or "mistreating" slaves than what else was going on among the other ignorant descendants of the brutal English royalty that had killed most of the tribes of American Indians and brought slaves from Africa to work for them as non-human assets.

This important research by current students that no one properly carried out before shows that the university was built on the backs and the blood of the slaves. Trustees and the rich donated money but it was often from trade slaves. Former claims by the university and some of the current members who denied such a trade slave helping found the university are another form of disclaimers of slavery. These are the same descendants of brutal British who founded this nation of liberty, justice and freedom for not all but those carefully chosen. All these continues to reflect in the racism of this country as it continually shows fascination for the current Royals who acquired false respect of the descendants of those Trustees and others and their children or descendant who learned to be racist.

• • • • • • • • • •

References
-Penn & Slavery Project, www.pennandslaveryproject.com
-Penn & Slavery Project, www.dp.com
-Penn & Slavery Symposium, www.thedp.com
-Penn Students Expose Universities Early Connection to Slavery, www.phillymag.com

There are other universities and institutions at that time who participated in slavery but Penn's proximity to where the slave trade was brought in and grew across the nation is significant to mention here.

Other universities indicate similar experiences and benefitted also from labor of the slaves. Penn also used bodies of the dead slaves for research in very cruel manner. Some bodies were dug out of the graves and cut open in pieces to learn and the students then participated in it.

Penn's medical school was deeply involved in such atrocities. They owned slaves and promoted racist ideologies. Enslaved people worked on land owned by the university. Trustees who were children and descendants of British pirates and so called "soldiers" and "rulers" of the British Empire; they were involved in the same sordid activities with the slaves whom they considered equally inferior as their forefathers.

(This is a little real life experience for me after graduating from Penn. Dean Holmes Perkins always mentored me there. On my graduation he told me that I was given a teaching job on his recommendation at the School of Architecture in Alabama. I mentioned this to some of my friends who were much older than me and providing me a lot of help with housing and mobility when I did not earn anything much as a student. When I mentioned that I had this golden opportunity as a graduate to teach in Alabama, they just stared at me and said that was not a good place to go for me because of the wild animals and the huge mosquitoes that can cause many problems to me. Well, later on in life I realized that they were just scared about my safety as a brown skin man from India in Alabama still struggling with governor George Wallace's racial divides and the riots that took place in the late sixties and early seventies. I was going to be very close to experiencing the racial divide and aggression towards my inferior origin and color as defined by the descendants of royals haunting America even now.)

• • • • • • • • • • •

"Princeton research project explores past ties to slavery" (Catherine Zandonella, Office of the Dean for Research) This chapter acknowledges their valuable and interesting research on slavery as practiced by one more of the many prestigious old universities in USA. After I graduated from Penn, I worked in Philadelphia and near historic Washington crossing as an intern in some non-creative architects offices. When I was admitted to Penn; I was also admitted to Princeton University.

Princeton University - Built by Slaves
Image: Library of Congress

I chose Penn for convenience. Princeton was on my mind and I decided to work for Professor Harrison Fraker in 1976 after our first daughter Natasha was born. We lived in an attic apartment above Harrison's office and I am not sure if he was really happy about that but Princeton was expensive and this is the easiest and cheapest solution that we could find. I slept and worked at least in an old historic building? Did I observe any blood stains of the slaves anywhere while enjoying living off Nassau street.

The research by students under the leadership and guidance of Professor Martha Sandweiss reveal facts of slave ownership among benefactors of Princeton University then known as College of New Jersey are similar to ones found at University of Pennsylvania my alma mater. The prestigious Princeton University formerly known as College of New Jersey was chartered in 1746.

This research reveals that the Princeton or College of New Jersey was not involved in retention of slaves but a lot of its benefactors did. The university was first located in nearby Elizabeth and then Newark and finally to its current location in Prince-Town which is known as Princeton now. It took its name as Prince-Town or Princeton University in 1896.

However, Nathaniel Randolph of British origin who donated original 4.5 acres of the land for the university owned numerous slaves. Several other donors to the university same as at Univ. of Penn owned and traded in slaves. They funded several of the university buildings. I loved those monumental buildings similar to British architecture in London and in some other colonies including India. I did not know that the buildings dripped with the blood of the slaves and the stink of the colonialist was infused in its monumentality.

The students from South were recruited and the anti-slavery movement at Princeton was relatively weak compared to peers like Harvard and Yale universities. Princeton became the place where people of vastly different ideas came together as per Professor Sandweiss responsible for this research material that I am using.

There are a lot of slave traders and slave owners among the trustees and donors to the universities. There were incidences of atrocities and discrimination of the highest kind including whipping of black residents. The most morbid fact is that New Jersey was one of the last Northern States to ban slavery and the universities like Princeton and the town kept its own secrets of slavery and brutality that are revealed now by recent students carrying out fabulous indepth research.

You can read colonial and British empire atrocities also in its monumental buildings built by the blacks living in Princeton in large numbers and the slaves owned by the trustees, donors and in some cases professors.

● ● ● ● ● ● ● ● ● ● ●

References
-Princeton and Slavery Project - Princeton University, www.slavery.princeton.edu
-Princeton Digs Deep into its Fraught Racial History, www.nytimes.com
-The princeton Slavery Project, January 2, 2020, www.muse.jhu.edu
-The Princeton and Slavery Project, online.ucpress.edu

Colonization Movement

Further to this research about owning slaves by intellectuals and politicians it is worth reading about "Princeton and the Colonization Movement" by Craig Hollander.

A lot of people in America and across the globe have not heard fully of colonization movement funded and supported by 19th century Princeton alumni. The ideas came from somewhat more educated and wealthy descendants of slave owners and traders to repatriate black Americans whether slaves or not to parts of Africa where colonies would be established. This mainly came about because some in high society did not want to carry on inherited guilt of slavery passed down from generation to generation. Americans even now fail to understand its significance as part of upper level society was saying suddenly that they do not need the slaves or believe in slavery any more and the Africans should be repatriated to some of the British colonies in Africa or the nearby islands to resettle. It also came about because of resentment by other southern whites living up North such as in Princeton or in Philadelphia "coloring" up their everyday racist existence. Colonization turned out to be partly an intellectual thought provoking idea more than practical. Some naturally started to manumitted their slaves rather than continue the hypocritical status. Some were reluctantly in favor of emancipation. Some were threatened by emancipation and what would happen to social hierarchy. Even today including me are conscious of their darker skin. I married two blondes my ex-wives and yet never somehow feel equal as often people asked where I am from which they never did to my wives until they heard their accents!!!! It is also interesting even today that Indians who are mostly highly educated are fine but not their black Amirican brothers. This is all because of British because in the colonies all over the world those of Indian origins were considered workers who were paid something or the other for work while the blacks were owned as slaves and had no rights. A slightly less dark skin even today makes a difference. I see myself invited to many parties and gatherings by whites but I hardly see any blacks specially in family or friendly gatherings. I have wondered why?

Descendants of colonialist decided to start abolitionist movement that failed. There were thousands of unprotected slaves that were an embarrassment to a few and thus they wanted them removed and settle back in Africa and these descendants of pirates and killers wanted them back in places like Sierra Leone. Some American statesmen of British descent began to decide to build colonies for free blacks on the coast of Africa.

Residents of Princeton were largely responsible and they led the colonization movement in USA. One of the 1797 graduate of Princeton University who was a slaveholder and trader was concerned that if the freed slaves remained in USA they would be unproductive and become a drain on local and national economy. That is Amazing because after all the slaves were brought from Africa to build and plough in the fields and they made life easier and richer for their masters. How, the free ones would ask for compensation and would be a drain on the economy????? They openly argued that white racism will prevent upward mobility for the blacks or "negroes". Yes indeed even now after more than two hundred years they are often neglected and they have limited upward mobility, higher rate of unemployment, less rights and justice overall.

Final contention in abolitionist theory was that the blacks or the free slaves will be prevented to achieve upward mobility by aggressive children or descendants of Colonialist. Yes walk thru the slums of Chicago.

The colonialist among themselves knew that this would happen and the blacks would unconditionally suffer and remain among the poor population of wealthy nation in which equality, justice and freedom was promised for all. Or may be not yet in my life time!!!!Colonization movement seriously thought that the best means or option to avoid conflicts and protect safety of whites or racist "whities" was to send free blacks mainly to Africa where they can establish their own "society" and than the whites can live happily and enjoy the wealth that the slaves free or enslaved had created. Amazing, incredible racism that still persist in one form or the other in good old USA even today. Detroit and every large city and its clearly evident that the blacks have been denied the opportunity for upward mobility and they remain the lower income population of America even today. They also believed that the free slaves would initiate race wars and thus become threat to their racially divided and designed public order. The race wars such as in Haiti at that time eventually occurred as well as emergence of leaders among them such as Martin Luther King who demanded justice and equality. During the race, riot and marches as recently as 1960's the blacks were treated like animals including by governor of one of the racist state Georgia openly.

Martin Luther King
Image: Library of Congress

References
-American Colonization Society, www.britannica.com
-Colonization Movement, www.philadelphiaencyclopedia.org
-How a movement to send free slaves to Africa created Liberia, www.history.com

This was also thought about it to keep the domestic slaves to work for the whites while letting go the useless free slaves who were unnecessarily coloring up their communities and the living environment. There was fear that the free blacks at that time would threaten the racial hierarchy and may be threaten their whole pure white dominated systems.

Some of the ACS members who were believed to be antislavery believed that repatriating free slaves would be humane and long term solution that would appeal to the slaveholders and those who were just using slaves but not owning them. Repatriating slaves was a sadistic idea for those who wanted to gradually abolish slavery and than live free of the fact that they had used and abused the slaves at home and in their business for decades. They also thought that slaveholders would be encouraged to emancipate slaves, as the newly freed slaves will not be staying in the country (let alone in the vicinity of all white communities). This would allow indefinite use of domestic slaves while letting the extra free slaves no one wanted to leave (another sadistic thought by British and their now American descendants who brought the slaves here in the first place while knowing all along that repatriation to African colonies selected by them would be equally harmful, painful and deathly to the so called free slaves). The religious leaders in ACS and otherwise also had an ulterior motive. The creations of colonies of these free American slaves in Africa would also export Christianity and spread of Christianity in Africa. How sadistic religious leaders had become. Sending back of the free slaves was like letting your work donkey or dog go so you don't have to worry about him any more while thinking how Christianity could spread in Africa or in any of the colonies. They also thought on the positive side because this could discourage in future African slave trade and the African Americans could learn to self-govern themselves. Wow, freedom at last.

In the senate, one of prestigious Princeton alumni, as per the student research, Samuel Southland of New Jersey (1804) became an ardent proponent of colonization. "Humanity and Justice," he exclaimed in 1830, "exult in the belief, that the gradual emancipation of the slave, and restoration of the free to the land of their fathers, may yet afford a remedy (to the evil of slavery)." Wow, finally a confession by the descendants of the British while now pushing or throwing the slaves out back into the sea to travel thousands of miles across the ocean to where the slave traders thought they should go without any choice.

Shorty after, President James Monroe put Thomson in charge of freeing slaves who were brought illegally into the United States. Wow, I thought all slaves were captured and brought in by the British slave traders here illegally.

This resulted in Thompson partnering with ACS to begin repatriating "victims" of the illegal slave trade (were there any beneficiary of the slave trade and how ?). I believe all slaves were dragged in horrible conditions across the globe by horrific acts of colonialist who wanted free work force and nothing else.

(Pamphlet supporting the American Colonization Society, published in Response to "the ardent opposition" of "some of our white citizens, and by a number of the free coloured population.")

Despite the efforts of politicians and the government officials, the colonization process began with the disasters for unfortunate free slaves. The first black colonists sailed from New York to Africa in 1820. They made a courageous attempt to settle in marshes of Sherbo Island, which did not even have potable water. Great ugly job by ACS who could care less. 49 of the 86 essentially brought here by no choice of their own died forcing the others to flee to Sierra Leone.

The next move was to move the slaves to Cape Mesurado. Local King at gun point was required (such as British had done everywhere in Africa and the islands disgustingly) to give the British Americans 200 miles long strip of coastal land which was then inhabited by 3,000 slaves over a period of six years.

British made this land also as if their own kingdom and named it "Liberia" These slaves built 400 farms along the coast and also built six schools on instructions of the monsters from prestigious Princeton. Oh, so these is from where the current rubber comes profiting even current day Americans who enjoy their rubber care tires!!!

Stockton and others in Princeton – along with the college and the religious institutes – persisted in colonization movement and its "philosophical" explanations. In 1850, as the tensions grew between the South and the North Stockton proclaimed :

"Let the great heart of Christian benevolence in the North and the South unite in selecting ….the proper subjects to be sent upon the missions of redemption to the land of their ancestors, until the last slave shall be departed." Of course when he says departed he means deported because most of the free or not free slaves were born in the USA and considered themselves American. They had no connection with Africa and nor had they ever seen land of the fore fathers.

Another active participant Professor John Mclean Jr. a complete racist descendant of the British occupiers raised money for voyages of the slaves and even recruited student body and faculty.

One should be nothing but ashamed of such a past long time ago but this research is very recent carried out by the students and even now many deny that it ever happened. Racism is nothing but racism or you can call it colonization to throw them back where they came from mercilessly.

The slaves were smart enough to know that throwing a few of them out will continue the slavery in the United States. The ACS chapter while working to send some to the colonies was reinforcing the slavery in the United States. In reality only 10,500 black Americans known as slaves or free slaves emigrated or were sent to Liberia. The colonization for all practical reasons turned out to be an intellectual exercise rather than practical option for blacks. This is why we have blacks and as the colonial whites predicted they are free now but carry a lesser standard of economic living and progress. The racial strife in one form or the other continues in USA even today.

● ● ● ● ● ● ● ● ● ●

References
-Princeton & Slavery / Princeton and the Colonization Movement, www.slavery.princeton.edu
-Colonization Movement, slavery.ptsem.edu

EXPLICIT RACISM IN USE OF SLAVES IN OTHER COUNTRIES AND NOT IN ENGLAND

British brought slaves – Africans, Indians and others – to large and small countries to use them for cheap or largely unpaid labor. Even in Guyana they brought people from India. One of my friend from Guyana looks like but denies being Indian and only reluctantly admits that her forefathers were brought from India as slaves but British often refer to them as workers to distinguish them from African slaves or local natives. England was kept pure by not bringing those low level races as British clearly tries to keep their "royal" or better blood from intermingling or creating mixed race in their own country.

The African slave trade
Image: The New York Public Library

They never mixed their blood with natives or those whom they traded as slaves across the globe. In a way women were mostly safe from low life ex criminal British soldiers. They had such inbuilt insulated feeling about the natives and that kept the native women mostly safe and not because the British were respectful. The British Royal bureaucrats in the past were all white. Now, because the British population is highly colored, parliament for the first time is full of other nationals where British ruled once harshly.

• • • • • • • • • • •

References
-Black Lives in England, www.historicengland.org
-The history of British slave ownership, www.theguardian.com

How did Puritans Plan for Politics and Native relations

The Puritans arrived in New England with a Mayflower concept. However, divisions begin to develop within the group. They were influenced by Calvinist theology, which believed in just almighty God. They also at first tried to convert the local natives who lived separately. Under Puritan belief some questioned the theft of native land but eventually that became the game and the natives had to be removed or eliminated. Puritans culture was like a cult and Salem witch hunt and other incidences seem to magnify such a belief.

• • • • • • • • • • •

British murderous occupation of Zimbabwe – Diamonds are girls best friends or that of British

(see socialistworker.co.uk from which following was written for fact checks and details)

When French, Dutch or Spaniards colonized or occupied any small islands or territories abroad they tried to mostly respect a lot of the native culture and people. They traded and ruled but did not carry out unnecessary massacre and torture to achieve their goals. They negotiated with the native people and even accepted the local culture, habits and even food. This is how the French learned to eat snails and introduced them to the world as Escargo when they were in West Africa.

British cruel rule of Zimbabwe lasted for a hundred years and ended in 1980. This was one of the colonies that was longest occupied among African colonies. The reason just like they say "diamonds are girls best friends" so they are also of horrific low life British colonialist. White minority in Zimbabwe had hard time giving up Zimbabwe. British profited hugely from mining and farming both using cheap local labor that was used in the cruelest possible manner. Approximately, 225,000 whites ruled without mercy and murder over five million natives. 70 percent of the fertile land was owned by 5 percent of the whites at the time of independence.

During the colonial rule of a hundred years the country was known as Rhodesia named after one of the most singular British Lord Cecil Rhodes. There were Dutch settlers and the British.

South Africa was essentially colonized by Dutch settlers who were equally murderous as the British. They had similar interest in diamonds and precious metals mining.

Cecil Rhodes bought rights to the mines or occupied most of the land by force. He formed his own company British South Africa Company with his own separate army that shot and killed any natives they chose like rats. The natives were whipped and enslaved and made to work in inhuman conditions deep underground with very primitive and unhealthy conditions. Rhodes had ambitions greater than the Queen. He wanted to expand the territories. British now had invented a new weapon, a murderous Maxim machine gun. In the battle of Shanghai 1500 natives were mopped down in no time while Rhodes army only suffered four casualties. Even some other blood sucking royals were shocked at such atrocities by Rhodes but he was essentially exonerated by the British Liberal Party. Once Rhodes had killed and acquired what he and the British wanted everything seemed to be acceptable. No form of atrocities was too much as Rhodes and the British colonialist as well as Dutch got rich on the mining in South Africa in general. They were not there to improve the lives of the natives and reduced it to nothing in no time.

Africa was extremely desirable because of its riches in mining and farming both with almost free labor available at their disposal. According to Historian Thomas Pakenham whose father was a British Penultimate Secretary describes the process in The Scramble for Africa as "Africa was sliced up like a cake, the pieces swallowed by five rival nations – Germany, Italy, Portugal, France and Britain " Rhodes ruled Zimbabwe ushering in brutal "compound system" for natives, effectively a prison camp for workers that continued in some form or the other until independence. The racist ideology of Britain and its imperialism provided for future white racist settlers from other places.

First and second world war ruined the British and this is why they let go of their rule in Africa. The American imperialist were now interested and they got involved in trades and other forms of subjugations.

● ● ● ● ● ● ● ● ● ● ●

References
Zimbabwe/South African History Online,www.sahistory.org.sa

Five of the worst atrocities carried out by the British Empire According to INDEPENDENT news

There is divided opinion among the current British citizens about British Empire. When the current British population is asked if the British Empire was a good thing; only 43 percent thought the British Empire was a good thing and 44 per cent were proud of Britain's history of colonialism as per YouGov poll carried out in 2016. There is a lot of hypocrites specially among the old generation and one of my friend actually finds current monarchy beautiful, charming and dreamlike to enjoy in this current technocratic world. However, who thinks of those who were starved and killed so that Britain could prosper at all cost? Following are prominent examples of the recorded atrocities across the globe.

● ● ● ● ● ● ● ● ● ● ●

1. Boer Concentration Camps

During the second Boer War 1899-1902, the British actually created concentration camps rounding up large number of Boers and keeping them like animals which resulted in outbreaks of disease and near starvation of the sixth of the population of Boers. Out of more than 100,000 interned in such camps about 27,000 Boers died along with 27,000 plus black Africans.

Boer War
Image: Getty Museum

● ● ● ● ● ● ● ● ● ● ●

References
-Concentration camps in the South African War?the conversation.com
-Women and Children in White Concentration Camps, www.sahistory.orgza
-Boer War:Haunting Photos of History's First Concentration Camps, allthatinteresting.com

2.   Amritsar Massacre

Peaceful protesters of Amritsar defied an order to disperse when they protested against the British Colonialist who were pillaging them day after day. On 13th April, 1919 (about a hundred years ago on the day that I was writing this) the protesters were blocked inside the walled Jallianwala Gardens and fired upon by Gurkhas employed under the British rule (British often used locals to do their dirty bloody work). Brigadier Reginald Dyer was in charge that day. Under Dyer's orders Gurkhas fired all their ammunition for 10 minutes emptying their guns killing about 1,000 unarmed innocent protesters and injuring another 1,000 within a period of 10 minutes only. Brigadier Dyer was praised by the British public back home and in India and they raised 26,000 British pounds for him then about hundred years ago worth a fortune now. This was a British popular response to a massacre of Indian protesters. This shows the kind of environment that existed then and everyday atrocities of killing a few more for any reason at all were common and rejoiced.

●   ●   ●   ●   ●   ●   ●   ●   ●   ●

References
-The Amritsar Massacre/History Today, www.historytoday.com
-Jallianwala Bagh Massacre/Causes,History & Significance,www.britannica.com

3.   Mau Mau Uprising

During Mau Mau uprising during 1952 to 1960 in British Kenya Colony; the Kenya Land and Freedom Army revolted against the colonial rule in Kenya. This did help eventually to free Kenya of the British colonial rule. The uprising was directed against the British occupation but it was cleverly turned into a war between the rebels and the African loyalist to the British. How clever. The definition of Mau Mau as provided by the British was "to intimidate someone" like mau-mauing someone. How clever and innocent on part of the British. They were unnecessarily being mau maued for occupying a foreign land and robbing it blind!! Poor "royal blooded" British.

According to the British who created a lot of stories and myths, Mau Mau mostly made up of Kenyan farmers was a secret society according to white occupiers who had earlier forced them out of their farms. Now the Mau Mau as they were called by their occupying masters were fighting to get their land and livelihood back and of course the followers of royal farmers or the superior race did not like any of it. Instead of whites fighting them they used the native Kenyans to fight them by telling everyone that Mau Mau was some kind of secret society to be frightened about.

Mau Mau were nothing but a group of fighters for the Kikuyu tribe that had lost their land to the British and other white occupiers. Kikuyu is Kenya's major tribe.

British South Africa Company
Image: Public Domain

• • • • • • • • • •

References
-What was the Mau Mau uprising? www.iwm.org.uk
-Mau Mau (1952-1960) www.BlackPast.org
-The Mau Mau Rebellion, www.bu.edu
-We are the Mau Mau:Kenyans share stories of torture,www.aljazeera.com

4.   Famines in Ireland - British Atrocities in Ireland

According to a reported article in INTERNATIONAL Action Center written by Christian Noakes "the film "Black 47" is a dramatization of the ethnic cleansing of Ireland. In Ireland it is known as "An Gorta Mor – the Irish Famine". It is so incredible and surprising to see British royalty thinking of even the blondes and red heads in Ireland not worthy of anything. Between 1845 to 1851, the King and the Queen then allowed 1 million people to starve in the potato famine called Gorta Mor and about 1.5 million were forced to flee hungry and sick to America and elsewhere leaving their cherished country and land. It is called Potato Famine but Irish were not only eating potatoes or only growing that one vegetable. They were growing other foods but it was exported to British as cost of imperialism. British backed landlords got the food or for export to British markets. Tons of grains were exported from the most famine impacted farm lands; writes Christine Kinealy in "The Great Irish Famine : Impact, Ideology, and Rebellion"

Also, as the film Black 47 shows the food was often taken at gunpoint as in other developing parts of the world. The Irish had little to eat.

British landlord and Royalty thought they did not want to encourage inferiority of the Irish which they blamed for the famine and the general crisis. British also similarly refused to provide medicine to the sick which they kept stored for their future use during the plagues across the globe that they often caused.

Queenstown, Ireland
Image: Library of Congress

● ● ● ● ● ● ● ● ● ●

References
-Great Famine/Definition/History,Causes and Facts,www.britannica.com
-Irish Potato Famine,www.history.com

5. The History of Indigenous Australians – and the British destruction

The history of indigenous Australians began when humans began to populate the Australian continent 65,000 years ago. The British arrived in 1788 and the disaster and killing of indigenous people began. British historians and other racist Australians claim that indigenous people died of an outbreak of smallpox and to a lesser extent of other diseases. Of course the British never touched them or killed them to occupy the Australian continent; yes we are gullible and stupid. They forget that the natives of Gweagal tribe opposed the arrival of the Captain James Cook. Some anthropologist suggest that the first humans who populated Australia migrated from the African continent. These early immigranst are not related to Southeast Asia or Melanesian population. The higher estimates logically place indigenous native population as about 1.25 millions. As many as 1.6 billion people lived as some estimate suggest over the life of the Australian continent prior to British colonization. The British killed them like ants and cockroaches and hid their atrocities. These many people but the British claim that they mostly died of diseases and ill care and no one killed them so by 1930 there were only as few as 50,000 aboriginals and now of course only a few thousand much less than the native population of Kangaroos!!!

● ● ● ● ● ● ● ● ● ●

References
-Who are indigenous Australians,australianstogether.org.au
-Inidignous Australians:Aboriginal and Torres Strait Islander, alatsis.gov.au

Most native humans were killed or died because no one gave them medicines for diseases inflicted by European settlers who brought them with them. While lovable Kangaroos along with killer European population thrived in lush green areas of Australia the natives were driven to the Great Sandy Desert as their last resort for survival. Indigenous Tasmanians were killed or driven to extinction. Very few original natives of Australia remained in small resourceless areas of Australia in small communities.

● ● ● ● ● ● ● ● ● ●

References
-Concentration camps in the South African War?the conversation.com
-Women and Children in White Concentration Camps, www.sahistory.orgza
-Boer War:Haunting Photos of History's First Concentration Camps, allthatinteresting.com
-The Amritsar Massacre/History Today, www.historytoday.com
-Jallianwala Bagh Massacre/Causes,History & Significance,www.britannica.com
-What was the Mau Mau uprising? www.iwm.org.uk
-Mau Mau (1952-1960) www.BlackPast.org -
The Mau Mau Rebellion, www.bu.edu
-We are the Mau Mau:Kenyans share stories of torture,www.aljazeera.com

Beginning of the reversal of fortune and the occupation of England now by "Natives and barbarians" as British called them

Now a days if you walk thru the London airport or thru the streets of London you essentially only meet foreigners. It's a colored community that the British named all over the world as barbarians. Barbarians are in their home now. As one of my friend, a proud very British Professor at the London University said to me "London is not England any more". Yes, it is also true that England is not British or the white racist Kingdom any more. It is full of those barbarians that the British occupied without a drop of mercy with extreme brutality. Now, the Mayor of London is a son of a Pakistani taxi driver. Yes, he is a brilliant attorney and deserves it but the main reason he got elected is because of the great majority of people who live and "rule" London's business world made up of foreigners; those barbarians from formerly occupied British colonies. Jaguar cars the pride of England's industry is now owned by an Indian industrialist family of Tatas! The British are losing control of Britain slowly but surely. This is also visible now in how the Royal family is changing and getting colored or even blackened.

● ● ● ● ● ● ● ● ● ● ●

Prince Harry marrying American actress – a great class and cultural shift?

In 1936, Edward VIII had to abdicate his throne just 11 months after becoming the King of England and the British Empire. His strong desire to marry his true love an American twice-divorced social-ite Wallis Simpson became a required mandate for his resignation.

Two decades later Princess Margaret abandoned her hope of marry-ing Group Captain Peter Townsend because he was divorced. The Royalty considered him unfit because he was divorced !! It did not matter that he fought for the Queen and he was a decorated World War II air force officer!! If you want to get down to bolts and screws of this matter; it did not matter that they were sexually involved!! Only thing they could not do is bear a child and ruin the long line of royal bloodline!!!! Isn't that amazing as now almost fifty percent of the people in Europe and here are divorced one or more times. Three of the Queen's children are divorcees. Prince Charles and Princess Diana got divorced which was one of the world's most publicized divorce. Is there something really precious about Royal blood or that they just made something out of their own ugly life? What a jerk Prince Charles must be to loose Diana. Diana was one of the more humane and social activist among the so called preordained and uncaring tribe of Royals. She seemed to be refusing to be part of the hypocritical royal tribe. She was doing her own caring for the world at a much higher level than ever demonstrated by any royals. Her honesty and sincerity had no impact on belligerent Prince Charles who was sleeping around with his mistress, now styled as "Her Royal Highness The Duchess of Cornwall" even while dating Diana. This dishonesty destroyed a decent and humane Diana.

350 million people watched Prince Charles and Diana get married. It was quite an elaborate public relation show to exhibit beautiful Diana with creepy Prince Charles who was already sleeping around with his mistress and pretended through the whole Royal marriage show. The show was staged to make the Royalty get as much exposure as possible and make them more popular which the marriage of beautiful Diana to creepy Charles did beyond their dreams. People talked about it across the globe and it gave failing popularity of the royalty a new boost. It became fashionable to follow Diana, talk about her and praise her as the world seem to love this beautiful adoring charitable woman. Royals got a huge publicity and boost to their Royalty thanks to a very humane and not so royal princess. I have always been in awe of her like most of the world. She showed to the world what Royalty of any kind could ever be.

● ● ● ● ● ● ● ● ● ● ●

Princess Diana and her Egyptian boyfriend

The world has seen Diana and her Egyptian boyfriend Dodi Fayed in photos in magazines and newspapers. This was not liked by the Queen or anyone among the racist royals. Their romance was admired by the world but not by royal ass kissing critics and news media in royal quarters. Everyone among the royals was brainwashed not to expect it. Finally this inter racial romance came to end in a fatal accident. Father of Dodi Fayed who owns a trophy store Harrods where the royals from across the world and the rich shop, he claimed for a long time wrongfully that his son and Diana were killed by individuals serving the royals in a conspiracy. This could not be proved. In some peoples mind it remains a suspicious mystery. In reality it was an accident as decided by the Scotland Yard and others.

The fact that during their own life there was no acceptance by the Queen or her useless husband Philip of their love and romance shows that the royals remained until then racist but the change is coming now with Prince Harry marrying a mixed race American actress. Some black blood hopefully in future children of Prince Harry will bring royalty to the reality of today's world. Prince Harry a rebellious young man may turn the wheels of time. Is Royal blood not going to be so Royal anymore?

• • • • • • • • • •

Marriage of Prince Harry and Meghan Markle, a mixed blood American

Looking back to the times of Prince Edward who could not marry his true love an American divorcee Wallis Simpson and had to give up the crown and almost his Royal self; one wonders what prompted the Royal family to agree to Prince Harry marrying a divorcee and a mixed blood low budget actress?

Is the dishonest insincere Queen under siege in her old age and has lost control of the not so Royal family? Is her cunning methods to sound superior and under control becoming a myth? Is the Royalty losing control? Is her diamond filled crown now truly becoming too heavy to carry and are those diamonds crying out of the pains inflicted across the globe? The early part of the last decade has placed Meghan Markle in news across the globe.

The Victorian Walter Bagehot once wrote "A princely marriage is a brilliant addition of a universal fact, and, as such, it rivets mankind" Prince Harry and Markle's wedding has been watched across the globe by a billion more than the wedding of then King Edward VII and Princess Alexandra of Denmark in 1863. The Royals often married Princesses available in other white northern countries thus keeping the so called royal blood and traditions intact. The venue remains the same; the mix of color and culture become remarkably different. Every young girl of whatever origin now can dream of marrying whoever without any limitations and girls of mixed blood and color must feel more confident of their origin. We feel that strongly when we see a beautiful blonde girl walking down the street with a black or an Asian man in all countries across the globe. The cultures are changing and the acceptance is growing. I am from India and I married a beautiful tall blonde from Finland in seventies when it was not so common. My daughter is now married to a Latin man and they received acceptance so happily among all.

Prince Harry will disrupt the streak of royal blood...wow finally the royal blood may not stink when mixed with black or plainly speaking African or negro blood. The change is definitely coming. I am emphasizing the race difference here because earlier the Monarchy showed tremors and shocks if anyone of their so called royal children went astray. They are left with no choice if you were to watch the persona of Prince Harry. After all Prince Harry is second born son of Prince Charles and adorable Diana. He is also fifth in line to the throne. Meghan Kelly has been a star of the television show in America "Suits". There have been racial slurs by media and other organizations. The gossipy mail once provided a comment that may be fit for this book in a way but essentially racist if left unexplained. They stated once " the Windsors will thicken their watery, thin blue blood and Spencer's pale skin and ginger hair with some rich and exotic DNA." Miss Markle's mother's upbringing through poverty or low income and other aspects of their family life has been mentioned as if they are a barrier to the vampire Royal British heritage that hopefully will be brought upon questioning once more people like me speak out. I believe that Miss Markle is doing a huge favor to the royals as she has brought humility but also a great publicity to the house of Windsors once again such as Diana did. The marriage of Prince Harry and Miss Markle was watched across the globe and will increase the northern American regards to Royals by a huge margin. We now hear how the Royals respect, endure and finally include "ordinary" people in their royal household. I definitely see the progress but I hope that this is genuine and not fermented out of absolute rebellion by a rowdy Prince. I hope that acceptance of Miss Markle is the rule and not an exception.

World is changing for the Royals and their tyrannical control is being lost in the new widening altered horizons of the world. They can not in a bogus way claim that their blood line is superior or based on those tyrannical British Lords across the globe just to torture, deny and destroy the weak and poor, as they did a century or two ago.

Just in a last few years it is becoming increasingly clear from the time of Princess Diana dating an Indian doctor first and then an Egyptian man that England must learn to live with time. The Queen can no longer masquerade Royalty and the Royalty is becoming more common at its very core. A son of Pakistani taxi driver can become the Mayor of London and Markle can marry the rebellious playboy Prince Harry.

London is mostly owned by foreigners. Most hotels and small businesses as well as large industries such as Jaguar and others are owned by Indians, Asians, Arabs and Africans.

This is why one of my more morbid English friend says "London is not England" and I say nor is Manchester or other such cities. Even the suburbs of London are teeming with foreigners and English have no place to create their own little enclave and stop occupation of England peacefully by foreigners unlike Brits occupying the world with cruel force using gun powder.

• • • • • • • • • • •

Queen Elizabeth's Jewels – Crown too heavy to carry?

On January 12, 2018, the Queen Elizabeth appeared on TV stating that whenever she puts on her crown she has to be careful as it is not comfortable. It is because of the weight of the diamonds and other jewels. She said if she does not keep her head erect and if she bends she will get hurt, fall down or the heavy crown will fall. No one on the tv or in any other news media mentioned that every diamond and all her very heavy jewels that she sweetly talks about were stolen from all over the world. Every precious diamond and emerald and all other precious stones were robbed and stolen with blood shed across the globe by her and her mother among vampire ancestors. Those jewels are dripping in blood of innocent people who were shot, hung or left to starve all over the world while the British Crown exploited and looted innocent people. Yes, this is why I have on the cover of this book her photo with blood dripping from her eye. She actually said it was uncomfortable when she wore it at her coronation but she did not say ever that she will return the jewels to where they were looted from by killing and mayhem. British snobbery is at display here in such a discussion and acceptance by over impressed media. She is really worried that the diamonds are heavy and burdensome. The interviewer is sympathetic to the fact that she is complaining about the weight of the crown. Well, give it back to the poor nations and people from where you pillaged and murdered to get them. What kind of suffering for queen mother is this?

Kings and Queens of the British Empire have stored crowns, jewels and other precious items in Tower of London and in all their palaces and museums. These items were robbed from their colonies dripping in blood or often presented by leaders of colonized nations or merchants to curry favors. This has been going on in the Tower of London for 600 years where tourist line up to see and admire them without knowing how much innocent blood was wasted by the British to acquire them.

Imperial state crown, King's sceptre with dove and jewelled state sword.

Image: New York Public Library

• • • • • • • • • • •

Don't Forget Slavery or Colonial Rule

In USA or anywhere else we must not forget the atrocious impact of the colonial rule and slavery brought upon by mostly British as everywhere. It has been often viewed as a glorified form of British rule and the British Empire. Even now there are people who remain under that rule and glorified enslavement. At one time it destroyed cultures, languages, independence and cultural values of a variety of countries. They enslaved them and taught them to wear essentially ties, eat with forks and knives and greet strangers with good morning, good evening and good night thus "eating" into people's private lives also across the globe and making them "civil" as the British will put it even now. This cold horrific culture ignored existing cultures and existing civilities of life.

Even today "the royals" old and young are playing this fake snob games. Look at Prince Charles. He is from another era. The young royals are playing it cool and considering themselves exclusive even if they went in England and USA to schools and universities like your and my children. A friend of mine went to Amherst with Prince Harry and they played polo. No one among the college youth thought of them as anything special but whenever the Prince went back to England in his snotty world, he turned snotty immediately. Look at the new so called Meghan the Duchess of Sussex married to "Prince" Harry. She became "Royal" blooded from mixed American blood. Her son is named "Archie Harrison Mountbatten-Windsor" Why associate an innocent child with Mountbatten? In his youth Harry as a single young guy did all the good and lousy things like drinking and dating; lied and cheated; studied some and wasted some days; and he is a Royal a Prince. How stupid and snobbish that is. Why don't the current Royal young people come out and say that their grandmother was nothing but one who created slavery and bludgeoned the world culture and killed innocent people across the globe. They should openly acknowledge it. They will get more genuine respect than this "royal" gig they are doing under great pretensions. In their hearts of heart they know they are the same as all other young people and they are kind of doing a job under the current Queen Mother getting huge sums of money from the British government and thus the people of England to live in the luxury of the palaces under pompous-greatest pretensions of any time in the history of the world. More than half of the British citizens are against such pretentions for which they have to pay from their pockets. Also, as the population of England is getting more complex and colored the chances of them continuing to pretend in those "royal" postures and positions are rapidly declining.

● ● ● ● ● ● ● ● ● ●

A question of Respect and Reparations across the globe

I believe that Germany acknowledges and respects the facts surrounding the massacre of six million Jews and the havoc that created in the life of the Jewish people across the globe. They agreed to reparations and promised the world that this would never happen. Germany has given millions of dollars to individuals, returned their looted wealth, paintings and most of the items claimed by the Jewish community as a whole and by individuals. Compared to that the British have failed to acknowledge their horrendous misdeeds across the globe. They have simply refused to return iconic, historic to the simplest of the items taken from public and private properties and individuals. They have often killed people if there was any resistance at all. No nation or even the smallest of the island they occupied forcefully in arrogance and with help of the gun powder have received anything back at all. Recently there has been a movement to get reparations in India to the individuals and the country as a whole but this has been largely ignored by the world. There needs to be an inquiry by international court and United Nations to look into the atrocities committed by the British across the globe and demand for reparations. Such demands have been ignored by the British Royalty as they believe that they did a favor by going all over the world to all the barbaric countries and taught them about their superior culture, civilization and their superior English language. They brainwashed the "barbarians" into believing that it was in their interest to be pillaged and robbed and taken over by their superior abilities. This looks like a repetitive "gulag" as they invaded some of the oldest civilizations and destroyed them at their whim. They did not allow the natives to choose, they essentially imposed their "superior" culture including the language on innocent people across the globe. The local people even learned to dress up like the British wearing three piece suites, ties and bow ties to win favors with their meager needs in the colonies. I still wear a tie and at one time wore bow ties and smoked a pipe to pretend totally as an upper class Englishman! We have all been brainwashed into their culture.

Huge number of English population continues to believe that they did a favor by going to all those "barbaric" countries which is ridiculous. I am waiting for their own country to be overwhelmed by people from those colonies taking over their businesses and livelihood. This has begun to happen and their lies the hope of the world in teaching a lesson in reverse.

● ● ● ● ● ● ● ● ● ● ●

British in Malaya

From an article appering in The Guardian "Revealed: how britain tried to legitimise Batang Kali massacre"

British were not only abusive during the ancient colonial times but also during the two world wars. Malaya is a good example of British atrocities during the recent times.

Malaya
Image: New York Public Library

During the second world war in December 1948, during the Malayan Emergency, Batang Kali massacre took place in which British soldiers killed 24 villagers for no reason at all. The British wrongfully blamed it on local people and the ruler Sultan of Selangor.

Usual lowlife british tactics which blame others. British General Harold Briggs at that time placed 500,000 men, women and children about ten percent of the local population in fortified camps numbering more than 400 camps. Thousands of their homes were destroyed and the local people forced to give up their land. The British were inflicting cruelty or in their terms punishment because locals were believed to be helping the insurgents. It was also to isolate them. Geneva Convention fully condemns such actions by occupiers during war but who could prevent God like British and their brutal soldiers trained to occupy, kill and destroy a nation.

● ● ● ● ● ● ● ● ● ● ●

References
-Malaya Colony-The British Empire,www.britishempire.com
-Malaysia - The impact of British Rule,www.britannica.com
-British in Malaysia/Facts and Details, factsanddetails.com

Hidden and burnt records

When British started collapsing their empire or moved out of a country they systematically destroyed all records. At one time The Foreign and Commonwealth agencies were hiding more than 600.000 historical documents in breach of the 1958 UK Public Records Act.

As the Empire was collapsing the British administrators in each of the colonies were asked to destroy those files that impacted royal image and British responsibilities.

• • • • • • • • • • •

Britain's Cruel and Crude Industrial Occupation - continues

Colombian State attacked for Industrial "occupation" by Britain

When British started collapsing their empire or moved out of a country they systematically destroyed all records. At one time The Foreign and Commonwealth agencies were hiding more than 600,000 historical documents in breach of the 1958 UK Public Records Act.

In March 2005 (as per Dan Read in London, July 10th, 2009), three trade unionists were taken by force from the poor shanty towns of Bogota. The soldiers of the High Mountain Battalions took them to the outskirts of the city and beat them as well as castrate them and killed them. The killings were disguised to show them as part of the routine combat operations. Such incidents have often been repeated with about 2,500 union workers killed in past 15 years. The paramilitary forces have been receiving military aid from Britain since 1980s to preserve their industrial interest.

Liam Craig-Best, a member of JFC has said:

"There is not one reason for the UK's involvement but a set of reasons as the two biggest foreign companies operating in Colombia are both British, those being British Petroleum and SAB Miller the brewing company – whose presence is much larger than the American and Spanish multi-nationals currently investing there."

There is no shortage of abuses by British companies taking advantage of the state of poverty and availability of cheap labor. There are other countries now involved in the industrial occupation of large and small countries across the globe. There are certain products such as rubber for tires by Firestone that come from west African nation of Liberia and United States industrial occupation across the globe is visible there.

The availability of rubber naturally growing in a country can result in a large American company such as Good Year and Firestone tires "occupying" most socio-economic and political "liberties" or norms of a small developing country.

• • • • • • • • • • •

Occupation in reverse – a process reversed or payback

The bloody English will be minority in their own country with certainty in about thirty years. Overwhelming number of immigrants occupy major cities of England such as London, Manchester, Glasgow and more. Foreigners mostly from former colonies occupy most industrial and other cities and small towns across England. Large number of immigrants now often more than several generations live in England.

When I was in London around 1970 most small businesses and small hotels were owned by foreigners. Now, gems of England's industry such as Jaguar cars are owned by foreigners. Jaguar is owned by an Indian industrialist and one of the biggest steel industry owner is an Indian but British citizen. Harrods a pride of English shopping is owned by an Egyptian whose son at one time was boyfriend of Princess Diana. And the list goes on. Foreigners are doctors, engineers, architects, BBC anchors, owners of large lavish and small hotels, large businesses and little grocery stores all through England. Many immigrants are richer than the locals. English have learned to cook curry and rely on services provided by former or current immigrants. Soon most of the England will be teeming with mostly immigrants from former colonies

• • • • • • • • • •

Racism and Colonialism or industrial occupation and brutality continues

Trump and his list of "Shithole" countries- Dark skin vs White skin? People across the world experience prejudices. Haitians whom Trump called as those coming to USA from "shithole" countries actually fought along the U.S. soldiers in the Revolutionary War and continue to be great contributors to the American democracy and progress. The prejudice against one's skin color whether brown, black or yellow has not disappeared. Silently the majority continues to believe in lighter skin color and light eyeball color. Blonde and blue eyes automatically represents an advantage as introduced to the world by northern European invaders in developing countries. Even in India or Cuba lighter skin is heralded. Rich women in developing countries often hide from the sun to keep their skin lighter. Who can blame them? The idea that lighter skin is superior is ingrown in most of us.

Trump recently speaking in Europe on July 15th, 2018 claimed that the "fabric" of Europe is damaged by immigration. We know that he is against immigration from countries other than northern European nations whom he wrongly believes as better contributors. What he actually means is that European fabric of citizenship is getting big dosages of "colored immigrants from developing countries and so the fabric is no longer white but from noble shades of white to the darker nonacceptable shades of brown and black immigrants. "Those are the color "patches" according to him which is changing the fabric of Europe. He as a child knew a white Europe that in his life has been colored by the coloreds across the globe. All you have to do is walk down the streets of London that Trump was not allowed to do because majority of the people in heart of London are a rainbow of colors and from a variety of small and large poor developing countries that Trump thinks are "shitholes" of the world. Trump as a child knew a white Europe that in his life has been colored by the coloreds across the globe. All you have to do is walk down the streets of London that Trump was not allowed to do because majority of the people in heart of London are a rainbow of colors and a variety of small and large poor developing countries that Trump thinks are "shitholes" of the world.

• • • • • • • • • •

Global Citizen – a great organization

While writing this, I was watching on September 29, 2018 Global Citizen festival in New York. This organization has raised billions of dollars and pledged to end poverty across the globe by 2030. They have given money, food, shelter, medicine and education to save and upgrade life across the globe. This looks like good beginning to create one universal culture across the globe.

• • • • • • • • • •

International Criminal Court

The courts across the globe have taken actions on every kind of torture in any and all country. However, their action has been muted when it comes to the abuse of international laws by the British not only in the past when such a court did not exist or even during the world wars. British seem to stay above the law. They have been only made to pay very small amount of reparations compared with what they have looted and whom they have murdered. Germans have been ostracized and brought to shame. Ignorant people in England as well as across the globe continue to glorify and romanticize the British and some other European royalties without thinking of the great harm and murders committed by them. One of my very British friend said it is romantic to have all that about royals in England and it is preservation of history.

How can such dark and bloody history be romanticized and placed on such a high pedestal? I know the British government likes it because of the tourists revenues it generates but think carefully. How can tourists from across the globe be so ignorant that they line up to wave and cheer the Queen Elizabeth even now and her pretentious husband Philip. How can young Prince and Princesses not know that their wealth was looted from across the globe and from drips of blood and torture. How can they as young people continue to pretend in this twenty first century knowing the history of their parents and grandparents?

How can they feel good about it even for a day or a second? They know the history. They are young and intelligent enough to face the truth and even challenge their obnoxious pretentious parents.

Do robbers and killers get respect in the manner in which the European royalty and specially the British royalty is looked at. It is time for British courts and international courts across the globe to study the atrocities of Queen Victoria, her ancestors and the current Queen across the globe. They should be taken to trials in the same manner as the Nazis and other such war criminals. We have to make the royalty in general pay for their horrible acts across the globe and find reparations and punishments without necessarily hurting the younger more innocent royalty.

• • • • • • • • • • •

Melina Mercouri and the Greek Marbles

Parthenon
Image: Pixelbay

Melina Mercouri was born in Athens, Greece on October 18, 1920. She became an activist very young in life besides becoming an internationally recognized talent as an actress. She was elected to Greek Parliament in 1977. Her autobiography titled "I Was Born Greek" was published in 1971. Later on in 1981 she became the first woman to hold a senior cabinet position as Minister of Culture. She was the first female in such a position. She got involved with all the European leaders to promote Greece. Restoration of history and its world renowned monuments became her priority. She strongly demanded the return of Pantheon Marbles to Athens. Parts of the buildings of Parthenon were savaged and looted by barbaric British and the marbles were sitting in British museums for the world to see without any charges against the British. Museums of Britain are full of precious stones from Kohinoor diamond as well as art frescoes and antiques. Historic Acropolis in Athens was savaged by British barbarians without any thoughts of the harm they were causing. The 7th Earl of Elgin was responsible for this. Miss Mercouri worked hard holding international competition to construct New Acropolis Museum in Athens where the marbles would be displayed.

Mercouri also commissioned a study for the integration of all the archaeological sites of Athens. She introduced free access to archaeological sites for Greek citizens thus increasing their knowledge of their cultural wealth and what was lost to the colonial powers. She supported restoration of buildings of special archaeological and historic building in Greece. During her second term in the parliament and she promoted creation of cultural park in the Aegean Islands. She created links to history and its interest in education. As one can see millions of tourists now flock to the Greek monuments and museums to learn about a remarkable historical era.

While I was a young student in London during the early seventies, Melina Mercouri the famous Greek actress raised voices against British asking them to return the Greek marbles meaning ancient sculptures and even parts of historic buildings placed mostly in London or in the British Museum. She failed to convince the crooked royals or the British Parliament retaining the precious historic artifacts removed from great historic sites across Greece. This is an example of insensitive looting and destruction of an ancient culture. British were essentially barbarians when Greeks were building currently preserved historic buildings and artifacts. Britain has no right to keeping any of the artifacts from Greece or from anywhere else and should return them all to each country from where they were looted . United Nations historic preservation agencies should demand it so some of the historic site broken and defaced in Greece as well as across the globe can be restored. Shame on the British who sent nothing but hooligans, criminals and vandals that they released from their prisons to help them increase their numbers and criminality in occupied territories.

Detail of the famous Elgine's marble frieze from Parthenon seen at the British Museum in London
Image: Internet Archive Book Images

193

Columbus Day

Really a Columbus Day that all Americans are supposed to celebrate!!!! Why because a drunkard ignorant sailor made a mistake and instead of landing in India landed in America. This resulted in occupation of this country for 200 years. After this he and his thugs that he brought set out to take over whatever they can and the British followers in the process killed and annihilated most of the Indian tribes and a huge population of Indians in Canada also. He ended up calling the native decent people minding their own business Indians because this uncoordinated fool thought and believed that he was in India.

CNN reported during this last Columbus Day in 2019 that the vandals threw red paint on the statue of Christopher Columbus in San Francisco. There were graffiti of course. The words were cruel but reflective of harbored hatred and inner feelings which essentially said "Destroy all monuments of genocide and kill the colonizers" I thought that is a bit violent but then Columbus caused rivers of human blood eventually and deserves that rebuke. The Indigenous People as the natives are being called by very civil white descendants of European occupiers were not happy. Why? America could have been occupied in civil manner without drowning hundreds of native tribes in blood bath and disseminating most of them so only a few token tribes and a small population of the original owners of this great land remain.

Many civil citizen groups have asked that the Columbus Day be rightfully now named Indigenous People's Day...........but who among the whites are willing to give up their false sense of pride in occupation by their forefathers. However, San Francisco is one of the city that observes Indigenous People's Day........wow I did not know that !!!! How about the nation declaring that to be the true celebration of indigenous people and making it official. Some say it was horrible to disfigure the statue. I say remove it like they removed horrific killer Queen Victoria's statue from across a railway station formerly named Queen Victoria Terminus near my high school in Mumbai. Many worried about our tax dollars for repairing the damage......instead of saying cut it up in pieces although it may bleed of native Indians blood but for being sane remove it. Please as one of the graffiti on the statue said "Stop celebrating Genocide"

● ● ● ● ● ● ● ● ● ● ●

Montgomery, Alabama

Montgomery, Alabama – a cradle of civil rights movement – was finally able to elect its first black Mayor in 2019 – a historic event showing power of old British descendants prejudices against blacks or negroes as they are still called often in racist Alabama prevented black leadership for so long. The reason is very simple. People in Alabama are descendants of British and other European nationalist who resisted emancipation and think of "negroes" even now as low life. These were some of the slaves brought by the British, While the state and its agencies may have adopted changes, the local ignorant racist population has not accepted the blacks. Blacks essentially live a separate life from the whites.

Hong Kong under control of British

Hong Kong remains under British control. The current strikes by students and others have resulted in nothing but aggravated strife for local Hong Kong population with no result. They actually would not be under Chinese rule if they were not bargained at gun point by the British who took over Hong Kong and then handed it back to the Chinese on July 1, 1997. Instead of giving the Hong Kong to the people of Hong Kong they placed it in hands of Chinese again.

It ended one and a half century of British rule but British created again devisions and established "one country, two systems" intentionally.

Hong Kong continues to struggle now for freedom from China. We all know how and what is going on. The world needs to come to help of Hong Kong and make them free.

• • • • • • • • • •

Royalty the Kings and Queens – Power struggle among themselves

The recent movie Mary Queen of Scots explores the turbulent life of a power hungry charismatic queen Mary Stuart. Queen of France at 16 by marriage, widowed at 18, Mary defies pressure to remarry and instead goes to her native Scotland to reclaim her rightful throne. By birth, she also has a rival claim to the throne of Elizabeth 1, who rules as the Queen of England. Determined to rule as much more than a figurehead, Mary asserts her claim to the English throne, threatening Elizabeth's sovereignty. Rivals in power and in love, the two queens make different choices about marriage and children. Betrayal, rebellion and conspiracies within each court imperils both Queens- drives them apart, as each woman experiences the bitter cost of power struggle. So called Royals have always been rival and competing even now for greater publicity and unresolved valor.

• • • • • • • • • •

Discredit royalty across the globe

I think it is time to discredit royalty across the globe. We cannot be so gullible or be fooled into believing that there is such thing as royal blood and they can do no wrong. It would be wrong to believe that the world benefited from their ravages and occupation. They did not "civilize" the world as some British authors claim. They looted, ravaged and destroyed the other cultures and did not allow the others to prosper and improve. They imposed their will by use of gun powder to develop a variety of cultures in their favor to wear ties, say good morning and good night politely while creating bureaucratic lifeless culture like their own for their own greed.

• • • • • • • • • • •

English Breakfast Tea?

This hoax was carried forward in other areas of life where anything orderly was named very British!!! Or English!!! It is time to get rid of their labels and myths from everywhere. It is mythological to think that any such tea or anything else produced by other nations for centuries which British looted or continue to make money from is English or British. Such a conspiracy of entitlement should be abolished at once.

• • • • • • • • • • •

American Indians and Reservations

The Americans in our time have believed that giving some of the small amount of land to a few surviving Indians and their tribes was their great heartful answer to pay them back. This is nothing but pretending. In reality all of the USA territory belongs to the few surviving Indians and their tribal chiefs. It's a pitiful amount compared to what they lost. They were killed and destroyed by the British and their lands were taken. We Americans are not doing them any favor by giving them isolated pieces of land. It is a shameful way of treating them "special" and thus separating them during the democracy from the remainder of America and its progress. Americans have not treated Indians better than the British did. They are free but isolated from superior white America. While America went through the industrial revolution and reservations smoking pot and taking drugs while remaining mostly uneducated. Most they have done is sold tobacco, cigarettes and alcohol cheaper because they can sale free of tax. The other thing they did is open up casinos with hotels in some locations and those tribes prospered but remain mostly uneducated. The families living on those casino reservations get check for doing nothing thus creating no ambition among the young or old to get educated and further their career or live in the society equally in the cities near them. One can write a book on this. Also, one can write how Americans created industrial occupation unfairly across the globe but that is not the subject of this book.

Princes Diane - Uniquely Royal

Princess Diane the darling of the world dated and slept with an Egyptian. I am certain that this burned up the Royals but they could not do much as Prince Charles chose his mistress. Prince Andrews mixed blood wife has brought better realization of not so royal blood among some stinky cheesy "Royals". So called Royal blood has begun to be mixed. Hopefully, this will bring liberation of such low life thinking about the others among the "Royals". Time to wake up and catch up with the rest of the world in this beautiful century where differences between people of all races are dissolving faster than ice bergs or anything else.

Bravo to the young across the globe. Our beautiful world is coming together and "royalty" in most nations is being derided by majority of the people. For the first time in more than 75 years we have not had any world wars. America is power hungry nation now and they kill people often with help of England and rejoice in power game and bombing other countries.

All across the globe young and old communicate with people of other countries and empathize with every individual on this planet earth. World is coming together who had learned to suffer under British. British divided and conquered. They created hatred. Its biggest example is how Churchill planned the freedom for India but divided it up in three parts resulting in murder and mayhem among innocent Indians.

● ● ● ● ● ● ● ● ● ● ●

British War Crimes

As per reports in general found on a variety of historical sites, the British war crimes were those committed by the armed forces of the United Kingdom. The laws and customs of war were violated since the Hague Conventions of 1894 and 1907. The British were brutal and also destroyed tons of records in many countries thus it is difficult to really place a number on it or even point a finger to any particular incident or individuals appointed by the Royals. Whether it was Queen Victoria or the current Queen Elizabeth, there were summary executions of "prisoners of wars" and others. Also, unnamed shipwreck survivors were shot and killed or executed.

First slaves for British West Indies were taken from this port, hence name of Cormantynes given to West Indies slaves from the Gold Coast. 1562-67."
Image: The New York Public Library

There was also excessive use of force during interrogation of prisoners of war and enemy soldiers. The violence was also committed against any civilians who joined any kind of rebellion as it is observed almost in all occupied land by the British. However, recent YouGov poll shows that 44 percent of British are proud of British history of occupation and destruction. Only about 21 percent regret it and the others fail to comment.

In 1922 when the current Queen Elizabeth was a child, the British Empire brutally and unchallenged ruled a fifth of the world population and a quarter of the world's land where there was anything at all to destroy and rob.

There were brutal massacres, use of concentration camps, destruction of old civilization and looting of their heritage. This is why it is wrong to give her any respect. It is time for Royals to apoligise and dissolve the drama around fake Royal blood, and royal titles.

• • • • • • • • • •

Anticipated death of the British Empire
and Royalty's decline and eventual emancipation

We can see the first signs of the beginning of the death of British empire and the England for British only as soon as you arrive in London Airport. The streets of London full of people from across the globe a lot of them who resettled from former colonies makes one think where are the English men and women. As one of my friend from the University of London put it "London is not England anymore" The fact is that a lot of England is not English or British anymore!!! The city is full of people from across the world from a variety of countries that British occupied. You see Asians, Arabs, Africans, Irish, Scottish and other Europeans. A world has descended permanently on England and not only in London but other large cities like Manchester, Birmingham and even small suburbs and villages. It is almost as if the world has decided that once the British cruelly occupied their countries and now peacefully they will grow and take England. I lived in London in 1969 to 1971 as a student and as an architect intern. Yes, the world and so the England has changed rapidly in the last fifty years. The pretentious, presumptive and obnoxious London does not in real life belong to England but to the people of the colonies across the globe whom British tortured. It is slowly being taken over by the people whom the British treated like slaves, tortured, massacred and looted.

London is essentially occupied by people other than English or the British. You can feel it now when you walk through the heart of London as compared to when I lived there. Now, the British are seeing their homeland being taken over. Instead of teaching Indians how to behave and eat at a table with forks and knives, Indians have taught them to cook and eat curry at home. I cannot help but laugh when I think of it. The English are now finally learning about the cultures that they openly despised. By 2040, the Anglos, the British or the English whatever you want to call these horrific race baiters and actual inventors of superior and inferior race designations, will be a minority in their own country. Hopefully they will be minority and inferior in achievements and developments as the other races will dominate all aspects of lifestyle, achievements and wealth. That as they say is truly a sea change happening right before our eyes.

I remember in 1970, one memorable day that stunned and shocked me. I was crossing Tottenham Court road in the heart of London. An old angry drunk miserable looking low life English crossing from the other side shouted at me "Hey you damn foreigners get out of here you ignorant primitive bastard". I was a student acquiring graduate degree in architecture and here was a low life British telling me to get out of his country. Slowly but surely all of us from different former colonies will take over not only their city but the whole of

England without even touching a hair on the head of the pretentious low life British occupiers. Now, that may feel great. A revenge without a single bloodshed in this finally enlightened beautiful world of ours.

Fort the first time the Mayor of London is a son of a Pakistani taxi driver a cultural and political impact greater than Obama becoming President. A lot of local politicians as well as those who sit in parliament are foreigners. This must be unnerving to those who think no one can touch their England. Actually, there are other major take overs. Jaguar car industry the pride of England is owned by Tata (I believe his grandson went in the same school as me in Mumbai....I think). Harrod's a legendary shopping center is owned by an Egyptian. There are hundreds of businesses and small to large prestigious hotels owned by foreigners and not by the English or British. Culturally, a son of an Egyptian dated emblematic Princess Diana. And now Prince Harry is married to a racially mixed blooded esteemed American woman. Slaves blood runs in her veins.

• • • • • • • • • •

MEDIA FEVER AND WORLDWIDE FASCINATION FOR THE BLOOD DRIPPING ROYALS – THE QUEEN AND THE ROYALS AS I SEE THEM COVERED WITH BLOOD AND NAKED WITH NO CLOTHES

American and Canadian media loves the Queen, the Princes and the Princesses. Every child born in this brutal blood sucking so called ROYAL FAMILY is revered and receives their highest esteem. Why? Aren't this the same people whose forefathers committed crimes on humanity across the globe. Are mostly white citizens of America and Canada who form the majority unable to accept the fact that it is wrong to cheer, love and give phony respect. When the Queen or a Prince goes to Canada or anywhere else in the former British colonies, part of the formerly enslaved population of the country or the "brethren" of the blood dripping royals come out waving flags, flowers and balloons. One wonders if they ever read the treacherous history, killings and lootings by this Queen Mother and her forefathers even in their own country let aside the rest of the formerly colonized world. Canada, Ireland and some islands by design are still part of the United Kingdom in some form or the other and the influence can be pervasive. However, I believe Canada has decided to give up on the Queen Elizabeth or any other royals being head of Canada in any manner and form once the Queen Elizabeth dies.

CNN and Fox as well as all other media in North America and elsewhere go ga ga any time the Queen or any other Princess or Prince appears in public or as an event such as the next royal is born.

If one thinks and knows that this current so called Royal family's forefathers were tyrants across the globe than why such love and reverence for royal members of the royal family. The royal tyrants were tyrants greater than Hitler. Hitler occupied six percent of the world, the Queen Victoria occupied sixty percent or more of the world for a long periods and took liberty to robe and kill as they pleased. Why anyone want to give them the slightest of respect in the twenty first century? For what? Even if fifty percent of the English population thinks that it is wrong to give the royals huge sums of money per year to maintain the lifestyle and shenanigans of the royals.

Why should the world care if it is Queen Elizabeth's anniversary or ignorant Prince Phillip's birthday? Instead of coming out in praise or even showing any respect, there should be a legitimate discussion about what this Royal family represents. Do they deserve any respect and love even if they are only the 2nd generation descendants of the blood sucking vampire Queen Victoria?

The crown jewels and decorations that they exhibit to look "royal" have been stolen by bloody force from across the globe. They are dripping the blood of people from across the globe. Time for them to go now.

● ● ● ● ● ● ● ● ● ●

Removal of Confederate Statues and Flags

In USA finally there is a movement to remove all confederate monuments, flags and symbols supported by street demonstrators, to the elite and politicians. Some of these confederate leaders were slave traders and abusers even after the slaves were liberated Queen Victoria and her family members and those cruel inhuman lords and commanders who destroyed civilizations across the globe and killed millions by their actions deserve similar faith. Royals should not receive any contrived respect. It is disgusting to see people bowing to the Queen and her so called royal family. They should be removed from such assumed positions. England should stop paying huge stipends to these pretending royals and remove them from those palaces and make them regular ordinary citizens without any fake royal titles and benefits. This will happen but it will take few more decades or years. Just the change in majority of population becoming non English will create the environment of no additional benefits and respect for the royals. It is already being felt as they are often made fun of and neglected or not respected by a large number of residents of England.

No one is Royal or above anyone because of how they were born to such killers and destroyers of civilizations. It is time now to begin the neglect and non respect.

Deep Sheathead Racism Created By The British Across The Globe

The British began slave trade around 1563 that lasted 245 years. Their poor treatment of not only slaves but others with different ethnic backgrounds has resulted in the deep sheathed racism created across the globe. There were no inferior, superior or royal people until British and other Europeans who went across the globe created the inferiority complex and neglect of what they called "the natives". Eventually, they pronounced themselves as not only the royals but blue blooded. They protected their lineage and thought of others not suitable to marry or become part of their family or community. This is why British never brought slaves to England but only to other countries including USA in large numbers. They also created civil servants in India in huge number and used them as "employees" across the globe to run their bureaucracy. Indians were somehow treated somewhat better than those that they called Negroes. This is how institutional racism developed and many countries continued to be burdened by it as the vestiges of colonialism and slavery or a sense of inferiority complex continue to linger.

This kind of deep sheathed racism is experienced by blacks until now. Almost up to 1960's, the black household workers had to leave certain expensive areas before seven in the evening of our beautiful city on the waterfront; Fort Lauderdale; the Venice of America.

When I arrived in Fort Lauderdale in the 80's the things apparently looked normal except that blacks even now do not live among the whites and are crowded in poor homes in undesirable satellite locations. This is true in most towns and cities across America and elsewhere around the globe. Thus, our experiences continue to show that racism persist and it is deep sheathed ever since British got involved in slave trades and established separate guidance and rules for the native "coloreds". This is deep sheathed racism that the British created and without any remorse they keep presenting themselves as Royals and thus separate and superior. It is time for all of the pretending to go and the so called Royals should step down, pay the reparations, apologize and give up pretending as soon as possible. We all must advocate change.

THE ROYALS MUST GIVE UP THEIR POSITIONS AND BECOME LIKE EVERYONE ELSE WITHOUT PRETNECE.

Image: Kaizer Talib, Author

Kaizer Talib was born two years before India acquired independence in 1945. During his growth period to becoming an adult he noticed his countrymen and women emerge slowly from being called "rats" by demonic Winston Churchill to becoming proud citizens of India. He could sense that his parents and grandparents who partly grew up under colonial rule would have made great strides if they were not enslaved by Queen Victoria and Queen Elizabeth. He emerged from similar understanding of what happened in other enslaved countries across the globe under the British Colonial rule. "Natives" as the

British royals called them were treated like slaves or worse and millions were killed, plagued or starved. This book depicts in words and photos the massacre across the globe caused by the Royals and demands apologies, reparations and removal of so called royals from their current fake status. He also talks about how British are also responsible for enduring deep sheathed racism.

Kaizer Talib is also a well known architect. His energy conscious designs in the USA and abroad have received awards and commendations. He is an author of several technical papers and a book on housing. He has been involved in alternative sources of energy, research and teaching on four continents.

kaizerdesigngroup@gmail.com

Made in the USA
Columbia, SC
30 September 2020

21829955R00117